flashcards and
quick questions

AQA PSYCHOLOGY
FOR A LEVEL YEAR 2
Flashbook

Cara Flanagan
Rob Liddle
Arwa Mohamedbhai

C000220637

Published in 2017 by Illuminate Publishing Ltd,
P.O. Box 1160, Cheltenham, Gloucestershire GL50 9RW

Orders: Please visit www.illuminatepublishing.com
or email sales@illuminatepublishing.com

British Library Cataloguing in Publication Data

A catalogue record for this book is available from the British Library

ISBN 978-1-911208-42-6

Printed in the UK by Cambrian Printers, Aberystwyth

12.17

The publisher's policy is to use papers that are natural, renewable
and recyclable products made from wood grown in sustainable
forests. The logging and manufacturing processes are expected to
conform to the environmental regulations of the country of origin.

Every effort has been made to contact copyright holders of material
produced in this book. If notifed, the publisher will be pleased to
rectify any errors or omissions at the earliest opportunity.

Editor: Geoff Tuttle

Design and layout: Nigel Harriss

AO1

AO3

Book-link

Y2/A Student Book
Pages 94–95

Y2/A Revision Guide
Pages 56–57

Spec Spotlight

Gender and culture
in psychology –
universality and bias.
Gender bias including
androcentrism and
alpha and beta bias.

Psychologists seek **universality** but **bias** may
be inevitable.

Alpha bias – exaggerates differences,
presented as natural and inevitable.

Example = sociobiological theory, male sexual
promiscuity is naturally selected.

Beta bias – ignores or underestimates
differences between men and women.

Example = fight or flight response – based on
male animals, assumed as universal.

Beta bias leads to **androcentrism** – non-male
behaviour judged as abnormal.

⊖ Gender bias in psychological research
validates misleading stereotypes.

⊖ Promotes sexism in research process –
lack of female senior researchers.

⊕ Reflexivity – embrace own biases as an
important aspect of research process.

⊖ Essentialist arguments are common –
biased views presented as scientific fact
(Walkerdine).

⊖ Can help avoid gender bias –
collaborative research in future (Worrell).

3

4

Gender and culture in psychology. Gender bias – *multiple choice questions*

1 Psychologists seek _____ but bias is inevitable.
  (a) Universality.
  (b) Generalisability.
  (c) Globalisation.

2 Differences between sexes are presented as fixed and inevitable:
  (a) Alpha bias.
  (b) Beta bias.
  (c) Androcentrism.

3 Ignores or underestimates differences between sexes:
  (a) Alpha bias.
  (b) Beta bias.
  (c) Theta bias.

4 Non-male behaviour is judged to be abnormal:
  (a) Estrocentrism.
  (b) Androcentrism.
  (c) Ethnocentrism.

5 Fight or flight response is an example of:
  (a) Alpha bias.
  (b) Beta bias.
  (c) Theta bias.

6 Walkerdine's study found evidence of:
  (a) Universality.
  (b) Beta bias.
  (c) Essentialism.

7 Suggests male promiscuity is naturally selected:
  (a) Sociobiological theory.
  (b) Biosocial theory.
  (c) Psychosocial theory.

8 Recognising one's own biases in research:
  (a) Reactivity.
  (b) Reflexivity.
  (c) Flexibility.

Answers
1A 2A 3B 4B
5B 6C 7A 8B

Topic 1: ISSUES AND DEBATES

Possible extended writing questions:

- Discuss gender bias in psychology. *[AL = 16]*
- Discuss gender bias in psychology. Refer to **two** topics you have studied in your answer. *[AL = 16]*

AO1

AO3

Book-link

Y2/A Student Book
Pages 96–97

Y2/A Revision Guide
Pages 58–59

Spec Spotlight

Gender and culture in psychology – universality and bias. Cultural bias, including ethnocentrism and cultural relativism.

Psychologists claim **universality** but many studies **biased**.

Example = Asch, Milgram replications had very different results outside of the US.

Ethnocentrism – superiority of own cultural group, others seen as deficient.

Example = Strange Situation, reflects values of US culture (imposed etic).

Cultural relativism – psychology's 'facts' only make sense in the culture studied.

Etic approach looks at behaviour from outside, emic is from within a culture.

⊖ Individualism-collectivism distinction may no longer apply (Takano and Osaka).

⊕ Recognise cultural relativism (e.g. attachment behaviours) and universals (e.g. emotions, Ekman).

⊖ Demand characteristics – arise in cross-cultural research, affects validity.

⊖ Difficulty interpreting variables – e.g. personal space, cultural meanings differ.

⊕ Cross-cultural research challenges Western assumptions – promotes greater sensitivity.

1 The belief in the superiority of one's own cultural group:
(a) Universality.
(b) Ethnocentrism.
(c) Androcentrism.

2 Emic approach studies behaviour from:
(a) Outside a culture.
(b) Within a culture.
(c) An objective outsider's perspective.

3 Psychology's facts only make sense in the culture studied:
(a) Universality.
(b) Cultural relativism.
(c) Ethnocentrism.

4 Strange Situation is an:
(a) Imposed emic.
(b) Imposed etic.
(c) Imposed exit.

5 Takano and Osaka claim this distinction may no longer apply:
(a) Independent-collaborative.
(b) Instinctive-coercive.
(c) Individualism-collectivism.

6 *Not* a problem of cross-cultural research:
(a) Demand characteristics.
(b) Challenges Western assumptions.
(c) Interpretation of variables.

7 Found evidence for universal expression of emotions:
(a) Ekman.
(b) Bickman.
(c) Milgram.

8 Demand characteristics in cross-cultural research affect:
(a) Validity.
(b) Reliability.
(c) Universality.

Answers
1B 2B 3B 4B
5C 6B 7A 8A

Possible extended writing questions:

• Discuss cultural bias in psychology. *[AL = 16]*
• Discuss cultural bias in psychology. Refer to **at least one** topic you have studied in your answer. *[AL = 16]*

Book-link

Y2/A Student Book
Pages 98–99

Y2/A Revision Guide
Pages 60–61

Spec Spotlight

Free will and
determinism: hard
determinism and soft
determinism; biological,
environmental and
psychic determinism. The
scientific emphasis on
causal explanations.

Free will – we are self-determining and can reject internal/external influences.

Hard determinism – all human actions have a cause.
Soft determinism – freedom within restricted choices.

Biological determinism – control from physiological, genetic, hormonal processes.

Environmental determinism – we are sum total of reinforcement contingencies (Skinner).

Psychic determinism – behaviour directed by unconscious childhood conflicts.

Scientific emphasis – every event has a cause, allows prediction and control of events.

⊕ Determinism consistent with aims of science – increases credibility.

⊖ Hard determinism not consistent with legal system – moral accountability.

⊕ Free will – consistent with everyday life – concept has face validity.

⊖ Free will – not supported by neurological evidence (Libet, Soon).

⊕ Compromise in the middle-ground position (soft determinism).

Topic 1: ISSUES AND DEBATES

Free will and determinism – *multiple choice questions*

1 Free will sees humans as:
(a) Self-interested.
(b) Self-determining.
(c) Self-deluded.

2 Behaviour directed by unconscious conflicts:
(a) Psychic determinism.
(b) Environmental determinism.
(c) Biological determinism.

3 All human action has a cause but people have freedom to make decisions:
(a) Hard determinism.
(b) Soft determinism.
(c) Free will.

4 Skinner suggestion that free will is an 'illusion' is based on:
(a) Psychic determinism.
(b) Environmental determinism.
(c) Biological determinism.

5 *Not* an influence associated with biological determinism:
(a) Physiological processes.
(b) Genetic factors.
(c) Reinforcement contingencies.

6 *Not* consistent with the legal system:
(a) Free will.
(b) Hard determinism.
(c) Soft determinism.

7 Free will is consistent with everyday life giving it:
(a) Face validity.
(b) Internal validity.
(c) Concurrent validity.

8 The middle-ground compromise in the free will-determinism debate:
(a) Hard determinism.
(b) Soft determinism.
(c) Biological determinism.

Answers
1B 2A 3B 4B
5C 6B 7A 8B

Possible extended writing questions:

- Discuss the free will and determinism debate in psychology. *[AL = 16]*
- Discuss **two or more** forms of determinism in psychology. Refer to **at least one** topic you have studied in your answer. *[AL = 16]*

Book-link

Y2/A Student Book
Pages 100–101

Y2/A Revision Guide
Pages 62–63

Spec Spotlight

The nature–nurture debate: the relative importance of heredity and environment in determining behaviour; the interactionist approach.

AO1

Nature – heredity, influence of genes on behaviour, innate influences may not all be present at birth.

Nurture – environmental influences, e.g. any experiences (including pre-natal), lifelong learning.

Cannot separate two influences so focus on relative importance on behaviour.

Interactionist approach – e.g. in attachment, influence is 'two-way street'.

Interactionism in mental illness – diathesis-stress model (biology + trigger).

Interactionism in epigenetics – change in genetic activity without changing genetic code.

AO3

⊖ Real-world implications – extreme beliefs in nature or nurture, e.g. eugenics or state control.

⊖ Confounding factor – unshared environments (Dunn and Plomin).

⊕ Gene–environment interaction – one's nature selects one's environments (niche-picking, constructivism).

⊕ Evidence for interaction – passive, evocative, active (Scarr and McCartney).

⊕ Nature–nurture relevant to other debates – both are examples of hard determinism.

1 Which of the following would *not* be included as 'nurture'?
- (a) Learning to walk.
- (b) Learning.
- (c) Experience.

2 The general figure for heritability for IQ:
- (a) 1.0
- (b) 0.5
- (c) 0.1

3 Interactionism in mental illness:
- (a) Diathesis-stress.
- (b) Epigenetic-stress.
- (c) Dizygotic-stress.

4 A change in genetic activity without changing the genetic code:
- (a) Epidemiology.
- (b) Epinephrine.
- (c) Epigenetics.

5 *Not* a form of gene-environment interaction:
- (a) Passive.
- (b) Provocative.
- (c) Evocative.

6 Nature and nurture are both examples of:
- (a) Psychic determinism.
- (b) Hard determinism.
- (c) Soft determinism.

7 A confounding variable in twin research:
- (a) Skewed environments.
- (b) Paired environments.
- (c) Shared environments.

8 People create their own nurture by actively selecting their environments:
- (a) Concordance.
- (b) Constructivism.
- (c) Coefficiency.

Answers
1A 2B 3A 4C
5B 6B 7C 8B

Possible extended writing questions:
- Discuss the nurture view in the nature–nurture debate. *[AL = 16]*
- With reference to **two** topics you have studied, discuss the nature–nurture debate in psychology. *[AL = 16]*

Y2/A Student Book
Pages 102–103

Y2/A Revision Guide
Pages 64–65

Spec Spotlight

Holism and reductionism: levels of explanation in psychology. Biological reductionism and environmental (stimulus-response) reductionism.

Holism – people and behaviour should be studied as a whole system.

Reductionism – breaking down behaviour into constituent parts, parsimony.

Levels of explanation – from sociocultural to neurochemical (reductionist).

Psychology can be replaced by a hierarchy of reductionism.

Biological reductionism – explaining behaviour at a physiological level, e.g. neural activity.

Environmental reductionism – learning reduced to stimulus-response units, behaviourism.

⊕ Holism can explain key aspects of social behaviour, e.g. de-individuation.

⊖ Holism is impractical – vague and speculative as becomes more complex.

⊕ Reductionism has scientific credibility – necessary in scientific research.

⊖ Reductionist approaches lack validity – ignore social context of behaviour.

⊕ Interactionist approach – combines different levels of explanation, e.g. diathesis-stress.

1 **People and behaviour should be studied as a whole system:**
   (a) Holism.
   (b) Interactionism.
   (c) Empiricism.

2 **The simplest explanation is the best:**
   (a) Parsimony.
   (b) Hegemony.
   (c) Alimony.

3 **A higher level explanation:**
   (a) Physiological.
   (b) Socio-cultural.
   (c) Neurochemical.

4 **Environmental reductionism reduces learning to:**
   (a) Stimulus-reaction.
   (b) Stimulus-review.
   (c) Stimulus-response.

5 **Explaining behaviour at a physiological level:**
   (a) Biological reductionism.
   (b) Environmental reductionism.
   (c) Psychic reductionism.

6 **The diathesis-stress model is an example of:**
   (a) A holistic approach.
   (b) An interactionist approach.
   (c) A reductionist approach.

7 **In ignoring social context of behaviour, reductionist approaches can lack:**
   (a) Reliability.
   (b) Simplicity.
   (c) Validity.

8 **Unlikely to be adequately explained by a reductionist approach:**
   (a) Neurochemistry of OCD.
   (b) Conformity in groups.
   (c) Genetic factors in crime.

Answers
1A 2A 3B 4C
5A 6B 7C 8B

Possible extended writing questions:

- Discuss the holism and reductionism debate. *[AL = 16]*
- With reference to **two** topics you have studied, discuss forms of reductionism in psychology. *[AL = 16]*

A01

Idiographic and nomothetic approaches

A03

Idiographic approach

Study of unique individuals, no comparison with a standard.

Associated with methods that produce qualitative data, e.g. case studies.

Includes humanistic psychology and the psychodynamic approach.

(+) Provides rich data – may generate hypotheses, e.g. HM.

(−) Lack of scientific rigour – subjective, meaningful generalisations cannot be made (e.g. Freud).

(+) A starting point in research – can lead onto a more nomothetic study.

Nomothetic approach

Produces general laws to enable comparison.

Associated with reliable, scientific, statistical methods, e.g. experiments.

Includes behaviourist, cognitive and biological approaches.

(+) Scientific value – standardised procedures, concern with reliability and validity.

(−) The loss of the whole person – overlooks human experience.

(+) The two approaches may be complementary not contradictory.

1 Study of unique individuals, no attempt to compare:
(a) Interactionist approach.
(b) Nomothetic approach.
(c) Idiographic approach.

2 Method most associated with idiographic approach:
(a) Experiments.
(b) Questionnaires.
(c) Case studies.

3 *Not* associated with the idiographic approach:
(a) Behaviourist.
(b) Humanistic.
(c) Psychodynamic.

4 *Not* associated with the nomothetic approach:
(a) Scientific credibility.
(b) Objectivity.
(c) Statistical analysis.

5 Example of idiographic approach in memory research:
(a) The case of MH.
(b) The case of HM.
(c) The case of HR.

6 Strength associated with idiographic approach:
(a) Production of rich data.
(b) Standardised procedures.
(c) Meaningful generalisations.

7 Weakness associated with nomothetic approach:
(a) Subjective interpretation of data.
(b) Lack of scientific rigour.
(c) Loss of the whole person.

8 One strength is that the two approaches may be:
(a) Contradictory.
(b) Controversial.
(c) Complementary.

Topic 1: ISSUES AND DEBATES

Answers
1C 2C 3A 4B
5B 6A 7C 8C

Possible extended writing questions:

• Discuss idiographic **and** nomothetic approaches in psychology. *[AL = 16]*
• Discuss the nomothetic approach in psychology. Refer to **one or more** topics in your answer. *[AL = 16]*

Book-link

Y2/A Student Book
Pages 106–107

Y2/A Revision Guide
Pages 68–69

Spec Spotlight

Ethical implications
of research studies
and theory, including
reference to social
sensitivity.

AO1 **Ethical implications of research studies and theories** **AO3**

Ethical issues concern valid, valuable research versus rights and dignity of participants.

Wider implications hard to predict, e.g. how research affects individuals and public policy.

Socially sensitive research

SSR – research with potential social consequences for people involved (Sieber and Stanley).

Important research, so researchers should not 'shy away' from this.

Concerns for SSR include implications, public policy and validity.

Example = Burt's research on genes and IQ had consequences for UK schoolchildren.

⊕ Benefits of SSR – promote greater understanding and reduce prejudice.

⊕ Understanding how to frame questions – avoid misrepresenting minorities.

⊕ Understand potential damage of SSR – e.g. subliminal messages (Packard).

⊖ SSR may be used for social control and prop up discriminatory practices.

⊖ Difficult to predict costs and benefits of SSR before it is carried out.

1 His research had socially sensitive implications:
  (a) Cecil Bent.
  (b) Cyril Burt.
  (c) Seth Blunt.

2 *Not* a concern for SSR:
  (a) Public policy.
  (b) Validity.
  (c) Reliability.

3 Researchers who identified concerns in SSR:
  (a) Slaby and Smith.
  (b) Sieber and Stanley.
  (c) Selwyn and Stokes.

4 SSR may be used as a form of:
  (a) Social control.
  (b) Social conflict.
  (c) Social contact.

5 The main focus of Burt's research:
  (a) Genetics and crime.
  (b) Genetics and personality.
  (c) Genetics and IQ.

6 Studied the misuse of subliminal messages:
  (a) Placard.
  (b) Laggard.
  (c) Packard.

7 SSR stands for:
  (a) Specially selected research.
  (b) Socially sensitive research.
  (c) Secretly sourced research.

8 Difficult to predict costs and benefits of SSR:
  (a) With limited budgets.
  (b) Because socially sensitive.
  (c) Before research conducted.

Answers 1B 2C 3B 4A 5C 6C 7B 8C

Topic 1: ISSUES AND DEBATES

Possible extended writing questions:
- Discuss ethical implications of research studies and theory. *[AL = 16]*
- Discuss socially sensitive research with reference to **two** studies/theories you have studied. *[AL = 16]*

AO1

AO3

Book-link

Y2/A Student Book
Pages 118–119

Y2/A Revision Guide
Pages 70–71

Spec Spotlight

The evolutionary explanations for partner preferences, including the relationship between sexual selection and human reproductive behaviour.

Sexual selection

Anisogamy – differences between male and female sex cells, sperm are small, ova produced in small numbers.

Anisogamy – results in many fertile males, fewer females, different mating strategies.

Inter-sexual selection

Females invest more in offspring so need to be choosy.

Preferences of both sexes determine attributes passed on (runaway process).

Intra-sexual selection

Males reproduce often as possible so compete for females.

Leads to aggression in males and preference for signs of fertility (youth).

(+) Research support (intra) – females value resources, males attractiveness (Buss).

(+) Research support (inter) – 75% males agreed to sexual request, 0% females (Clark and Hatfield).

(−) Ignores social influences – changing social and cultural norms affect preferences.

(+) Waist-hip ratios – males prefer 0.7, signals female fertility (Singh).

(+) Lonely hearts – women offered youth/fertility, males offered resources (Waynforth and Dunbar).

Topic 2: RELATIONSHIPS

1 Differences between male and female sex cells are called:
(a) Gender.
(b) Sexual selection.
(c) Anisogamy.

2 Inter-sexual selection is the preferred strategy of:
(a) Females.
(b) Males.
(c) Both sexes.

3 Inter-sexual selection is a:
(a) Runaway process.
(b) Static process.
(c) Cultural process.

4 A feature of intra-sexual selection is:
(a) Female preference for fertility.
(b) Male competition for females.
(c) Female competition for males.

5 Buss's research:
(a) Supports intra-sexual selection.
(b) Supports inter-sexual selection.
(c) Does not support either.

6 In Clark and Hatfield's study, what percentage of males agreed to a sexual request?
(a) 0%
(b) 75%
(c) 100%

7 Males prefer a waist–hip ratio of:
(a) 0.7
(b) 0.6
(c) 0.5

8 Women offered youth and men offered resources in:
(a) Online dating.
(b) Lab experiments.
(c) Lonely hearts adverts.

Topic 2: RELATIONSHIPS

Answers
1C 2A 3A 4B
5A 6B 7A 8C

Possible extended writing questions:
- Outline and evaluate evolutionary explanations for partner preferences. [AL = 16]
- Discuss the relationship between sexual selection **and** human reproductive behaviour. [AL = 16]

Spec Spotlight

Factors affecting
attraction in romantic
relationships: self-
disclosure.

AO1

Important early in relationships – sharing and intimacy, not too much too soon.

Social penetration theory (Altman and Taylor) – disclosing personal information is sign of trust.

Penetration – more deeply into each other's lives (more understanding).

Breadth is narrow to begin with – but becomes wider as relationship develops.

Depth also increases – more layers revealed as relationship develops.

Reciprocity – disclosure must be returned, not just depth and breadth (Reis and Shaver).

AO3

(+) Research support – partners who use self-disclosure more satisfied/committed (Sprecher and Hendrick).

(+) Real-life application – findings used to encourage couples to self-disclose.

(−) Culturally limited – less disclosure in collectivist cultures (Tang et al.).

(−) Link to breakdown – self-disclosure doesn't always save a relationship (Duck).

(−) Correlational research – not known if self-disclosure is a cause of satisfaction.

Topic 2: RELATIONSHIPS

Topic 2: RELATIONSHIPS

1 Self-disclosure at the start of a relationship:
(a) Is always unpleasant.
(b) Is always a good thing.
(c) Promotes mutual trust.

2 The importance of self-disclosure is explained by:
(a) Social penetration theory.
(b) Self-penetration theory.
(c) Inter-penetration theory.

3 As a satisfying relationship develops, self-disclosures:
(a) Become unimportant.
(b) Get deeper and broader.
(c) Remain relatively superficial.

4 The most satisfying disclosures are:
(a) Reciprocated.
(b) Only found in heterosexual relationships.
(c) On a narrow range of topics.

5 Partners who self-disclose are:
(a) Less satisfied.
(b) No more satisfied than anyone else.
(c) More satisfied.

6 There is generally less self-disclosure in:
(a) Collectivist cultures.
(b) Individualist cultures.
(c) The US compared with China.

7 Self-disclosure:
(a) Causes relationship breakdown.
(b) May not prevent breakdown.
(c) Comes after a breakdown.

8 Correlational research shows that self-disclosure:
(a) Causes satisfaction.
(b) Is linked to satisfaction.
(c) Is caused by satisfaction.

Answers 1C 2A 3B 4A 5C 6A 7B 8B

Possible extended writing questions:
- Describe and evaluate **one** factor affecting attraction in romantic relationships. *[AL = 16]*
- Discuss self-disclosure as a factor affecting attraction in romantic relationships. *[AL = 16]*

AO1

Factors affecting attraction: Physical attractiveness

AO3

Topic 2: RELATIONSHIPS

Symmetrical faces rated attractive (genetic fitness).

Baby face (neotenous) features are attractive – trigger caring instincts.

Attractiveness important in later stages of relationship as well as start/earlier.

Halo effect – we assume attractive people have other positive qualities.

(+) Halo effect support – attractive people rated as more politically competent (Palmer and Petersen).

(−) Individual differences – attractiveness less important to some (Twohey).

(+) Cultural consistency – some features attractive across cultures (e.g. Cunningham et al.), evolutionary basis.

Spec Spotlight

Factors affecting
attraction in romantic
relationships: physical
attractiveness, including
the matching
hypothesis.

Matching hypothesis

Choose partners of similar level of attractiveness to own.

Compromise – we do not seek most attractive mates, because of fear of rejection.

(−) Mixed support – original study (Walster) does not support, but later more realistic ones do (Feingold).

(−) Online dating – actual preferences are for more attractive partners (Taylor et al.).

Factors affecting attraction: Physical attractiveness – multiple choice questions

1 We find symmetrical faces attractive because of:
(a) Habit.
(b) Cultural pressures.
(c) Genetic fitness.

2 'Baby face' features are called:
(a) Neotenous.
(b) Neonatal.
(c) Monotonous.

3 Assuming attractive people are also kind and clever is the:
(a) Halo effect.
(b) Hello effect.
(c) Matching effect.

4 The matching hypothesis says we prefer partners who:
(a) Everyone finds attractive.
(b) Are the same level of attractiveness as ourselves.
(c) Are the most attractive available.

5 Physical attractiveness is:
(a) Unimportant later in a relationship.
(b) Very important to everyone.
(c) Less important to some people.

6 Attractiveness may have evolutionary roots because:
(a) It is independent of culture.
(b) Different cultures prefer different features.
(c) There are individual differences.

7 The matching hypothesis is supported by:
(a) Walster *et al.*'s original studies.
(b) Laboratory studies.
(c) Later studies of real-life choices.

8 People tend to prefer more attractive partners:
(a) In all circumstances.
(b) In studies of online dating.
(c) If they are very attractive themselves.

Answers
1C 2A 3A 4B
5C 6A 7C 8B

Possible extended writing questions:

- Discuss **one or more** factors affecting attraction in romantic relationships. *[AL = 16]*
- Outline and evaluate physical attractiveness as a factor affecting attraction in romantic relationships. Refer in your answer to the matching hypothesis. *[AL = 16]*

AO1

Factors affecting attraction: Filter theory

AO3

Field of availables – select field of desirables from this (Kerckhoff and Davis).

1st filter: Social demography

Social class, education, physical location, etc.

2nd filter: Similarity in attitudes

Sharing beliefs, promotes communication.

Law of attraction – attitude similarity is cause of mutual attraction (Byrne).

3rd filter: Complementarity

Partners have traits the other lacks, this is attractive.

Important later – gives partners feeling of togetherness, meeting needs.

$\oplus$ Research support – similarity matters but complementarity later (Winch).

$\ominus$ Lacks replication – findings not repeated in other cultures (social changes?).

$\ominus$ Direction of effect – similarity may increase over time as an effect of the relationship and not cause.

$\ominus$ Lacks temporal validity – online dating, demography less important now.

$\ominus$ Role of 3rd filter – complementarity not reached in all relationships (Anderson et al.).

Spec Spotlight

Factors affecting attraction in romantic relationships: filter theory, including social demography, similarity in attitudes and complementarity.

1 Physical location and social class are part of:
(a) Complementarity.
(b) Social demography.
(c) Attitude similarity.

2 The 2nd filter is:
(a) Social demography.
(b) Attitude similarity.
(c) Complementarity.

3 The law of attraction refers to:
(a) Social demography.
(b) Attitude similarity.
(c) Complementarity.

4 Complementarity is most important:
(a) At the start of a relationship.
(b) Throughout a relationship.
(c) Later in a relationship.

5 There is some research support for:
(a) Complementarity and similarity.
(b) Social demography only.
(c) Similarity only.

6 Predictions from filter theory:
(a) Apply to most cultures.
(b) Have been supported in most research.
(c) Have not been replicated in other cultures.

7 Thanks to online dating, filter theory:
(a) Lacks temporal validity.
(b) Has high internal validity.
(c) Is reliable.

8 Complementarity is:
(a) The 2nd filter of the theory.
(b) Not necessarily reached.
(c) Something all relationships eventually have.

Answers
1B 2B 3B 4C
5A 6C 7A 8B

Possible extended writing questions:
- Describe and evaluate **two or more** factors affecting attraction in romantic relationships. *[AL = 16]*
- In the context of factors affecting attraction in romantic relationships, discuss filter theory. *[AL = 16]*

Spec Spotlight

Theories of
romantic relationships:
social exchange
theory.

Theories of romantic relationships: Social exchange theory

AO1

Social exchange theory (SET) – economic minimax: minimise costs, maximise rewards (Thibault and Kelley).

Costs (e.g. stress), rewards (e.g. praise) and opportunity costs.

Comparison level (CL) – measure of profit based on level of reward expected.

Comparison level for alternatives (CLalt) – better rewards available elsewhere?

We notice alternatives if current relationship costs outweigh rewards.

Stages – sampling, bargaining, commitment, institutionalisation.

AO3

⊖ Faulty assumption – not all relationships are exchange-based (e.g. communal).

⊖ Wrong direction of effect – we only think about profit after dissatisfaction (Miller).

⊖ Role of equity – most partners find equity satisfying, ignored by theory.

⊖ Vague concepts – costs, rewards, CLalt, are subjective and hard to quantify.

⊖ Artificial research – lab-based games, real-life research is less supportive.

Topic 2: RELATIONSHIPS

1 According to social exchange theory, relationships are mainly:
(a) Economic.
(b) Psychological.
(c) Biological.

2 Relationships are satisfying when:
(a) Costs are maximised.
(b) Rewards outweigh costs.
(c) There are minimal profits.

3 Considering if more rewards are available elsewhere is the:
(a) Profit.
(b) Comparison level for alternatives.
(c) Comparison level.

4 The 3rd stage of a relationship is:
(a) Commitment.
(b) Sampling.
(c) Institutionalisation.

5 One type of relationship that is *not* exchange-based is:
(a) Work.
(b) Business.
(c) Communal.

6 Social exchange theory ignores:
(a) Comparison level.
(b) Relationship profit.
(c) Equity.

7 Concepts such as CLalt are:
(a) Easy to define.
(b) Vague.
(c) Straightforward to measure.

8 Real-life research:
(a) Is less supportive of the theory.
(b) Uses artificial tasks.
(c) Highly supportive of the theory.

Answers
1A 2B 3B 4A
5C 6C 7B 8A

Topic 2: RELATIONSHIPS

Possible extended writing questions:

- Outline and evaluate **one** theory of romantic relationships. *[AL = 16]*
- Discuss the social exchange theory of romantic relationships. *[AL = 16]*

Book-link

Y2/A Student Book
Pages 128–129

Y2/A Revision Guide
Pages 80–81

Role of equity

Both partners' level of profit should be roughly the same.

Under-benefitting and over-benefitting can both lead to dissatisfaction.

Equity is about fairness – the ratio of rewards to costs, not amount of them.

Consequences of inequity

Strong positive correlation between perceived inequity and dissatisfaction.

Equity should increase as relationship develops – reduced equity leads to dissatisfaction.

Inequity needs attention – restore equity (or change expectations).

⊕ Research support – newly-weds more satisfied in equitable relationship (Utne *et al.*).

⊕ Culturally limited – equity not linked to satisfaction in collectivist cultures (Aumer-Ryan *et al.*).

⊖ Individual differences – *benevolents* and *entitleds* less sensitive to equity (Huseman *et al.*).

⊕ Doesn't apply to all relationships – e.g. casual friendships (Clark and Mills).

⊖ Lack of increased equity – in a longitudinal study, self-disclosure more important (Berg and McQuinn).

Spec Spotlight

Theories of romantic relationships: equity theory.

Topic 2: RELATIONSHIPS

1 Equity means that both partners:
- (a) Get the same rewards.
- (b) Have similar levels of profit.
- (c) Get the same costs.

2 Dissatisfaction can result from:
- (a) A balance of costs and rewards.
- (b) Under-benefitting but not over-benefitting.
- (c) Under- and over-benefitting.

3 The link between inequity and dissatisfaction is:
- (a) A negative correlation.
- (b) A positive correlation.
- (c) Cause-and-effect.

4 Equity theory predicts that equity in a satisfying relationship should:
- (a) Increase over time.
- (b) Remain static over time.
- (c) Be high at the start of a relationship.

5 Equity is more important to satisfaction in:
- (a) Individualist cultures.
- (b) Collectivist cultures.
- (c) All cultures.

6 People who are less sensitive than others to equity are called:
- (a) Benevolents.
- (b) Entitleds.
- (c) Both of the above.

7 Equity is a limited explanation because it:
- (a) Is important only in some types of relationship.
- (b) Has no research supporting it.
- (c) Cannot explain profits.

8 The researchers who found equity did *not* increase over time were:
- (a) Walster *et al.*
- (b) Clark and Mills.
- (c) Berg and McQuinn.

Answers
1B 2C 3B 4A
5A 6C 7A 8C

Possible extended writing questions:
- Discuss **one or more** theories of romantic relationships. *[AL = 16]*
- Outline and evaluate equity theory as a theory of romantic relationships. Refer to social exchange theory in your answer. *[AL = 16]*

AO1

AO3

Book-link

Y2/A Student Book
Pages 130–131

Y2/A Revision Guide
Pages 82–83

Topic 2: RELATIONSHIPS

Spec Spotlight

Theories of romantic relationships: Rusbult's investment model of commitment, satisfaction, comparison with alternatives and investment.

Extension of SET – satisfaction is partners getting more than they expect.

Commitment = high satisfaction + unattractive alternatives + increasing investment.

Satisfaction matters less than commitment – avoid wasting investment.

Comparison with alternatives (CLalt) – judging possible other parners.

Investments are intrinsic (e.g. energy) and extrinsic (e.g. shared memories).

Maintenance mechanisms – keep relationship going (e.g. forgiveness).

(+) Research support – satisfaction, CLalt and investment predict commitment (Le and Agnew).

(+) Explains abusive relationships – investment and commitment outweigh satisfaction (Rusbult and Martz).

(−) Oversimplifies investment – not just current resources but also future plans.

(+) Self-report used – valid because model based on subjective judgements (e.g. satisfaction).

(−) Correlational research – factors linked but not cause-and-effect.

Theories of romantic relationships: Rusbult's investment model – *multiple choice questions*

1 Rusbult's model is a development of:
(a) Filter theory.
(b) Social exchange theory.
(c) The matching hypothesis.

2 One aspect of the model is
(a) Comparison of possibilities.
(b) Comparison with alternatives.
(c) Comparison of availables.

3 Investments are:
(a) Intrinsic and extrinsic.
(b) Intrinsic only.
(c) Nearly always extrinsic.

4 In Rusbult's model:
(a) Commitment matters more than satisfaction.
(b) CLalt depends on investment.
(c) Satisfaction depends on commitment.

5 Commitment is predicted by:
(a) CLalt only.
(b) Satisfaction only.
(c) The above plus investment.

6 Rusbult's model can explain:
(a) Abusive relationships.
(b) The complexity of investment.
(c) Short-term relationships only.

7 The model is based on research using:
(a) Lab experiments.
(b) Observations.
(c) Self-reports.

8 Correlational findings mean:
(a) The model is highly valid.
(b) Causes of commitment cannot be established.
(c) Commitment does cause satisfaction.

Answers
1B 2B 3A 4A
5C 6A 7C 8B

Topic 2: RELATIONSHIPS

Possible extended writing questions:
- Describe and evaluate **two** theories of romantic relationships. *[AL = 16]*
- In the context of romantic relationships, discuss Rusbult's investment model. *[AL = 16]*

AO1

AO3

Book-link

Y2/A Student Book
Pages 132–133

Y2/A Revision Guide
Pages 84–85

Spec Spotlight

Theories of
romantic relationships:
Duck's phase model of
relationship breakdown:
intra-psychic, dyadic,
social and grave dressing
phases.

Topic 2: RELATIONSHIPS

Relationship breakdown is a process – over time in four stages, not one-off event.

Each phase has a threshold – partner reaches point when perception of relationship changes.

Intra-psychic phase – dissatisfied partner broods on relationship's shortcomings.

Dyadic phase – discuss dissatisfaction with partner, varies in length/tension.

Social phase – 'go public', seek support from joint friends expected to take sides.

Grave dressing phase – produce 'story' of relationship so partners can move on.

⊖ Incomplete model – resurrection phase added, and also can return to earlier phases (Rollie and Duck).

⊖ Retrospective data – participants interviewed after breakdown, lacks validity.

⊕ Real-life application – can help partners cope with breakdown more positively.

⊖ How, not why – Duck describes process, other theories explain why (e.g. Flemlee).

⊖ Culturally biased – not so applicable to collectivist cultures (less easy to end).

1 How many phases does Duck's model have?
(a) 6
(b) 5
(c) 4

2 Each phase features a:
(a) Gateway.
(b) Brink.
(c) Threshold.

3 Thinking over the reasons for unhappiness is part of the:
(a) Social phase.
(b) Intra-psychic phase.
(c) Grave dressing phase.

4 The dyadic phase features:
(a) Discussion between partners.
(b) Telling friends.
(c) Producing a relationship story.

5 Rollie and Duck added a 5th phase called:
(a) Deselection.
(b) Restoration.
(c) Resurrection.

6 Research studies are flawed because they:
(a) Are conducted in laboratories.
(b) Rely on retrospective data.
(c) Are unethical.

7 Duck's theory is good at:
(a) Identifying reasons for breakdown.
(b) Describing breakdown.
(c) Explaining breakdown.

8 Duck's theory applies well to:
(a) Individualist cultures.
(b) Collectivist cultures.
(c) Most cultures.

Topic 2: RELATIONSHIPS

Answers
1C 2C 3B 4A
5C 6B 7B 8A

Possible extended writing questions:

- Discuss **two or more** theories of romantic relationships. *[AL = 16]*
- Outline and evaluate Duck's phase model of relationship breakdown. *[AL = 16]*

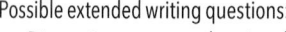

Spec Spotlight

Virtual relationships in social media: self-disclosure in virtual relationships; effects of absence of gating on the nature of virtual relationships.

Self-disclosure

Is crucial in FtF relationships, so what about computer mediated communication (CMC)?

Reduced cues theory (RCT) – less disclosure in CMC because nonverbal cues reduced.

Hyperpersonal model (HM) – early disclosure leads to intense relationships that may start and end quickly.

Possible to manipulate self-image in CMC, leading to more disclosure.

⊖ RCT lacks support – cues in CMC, just different from face-to-face (e.g. emojis).

⊕ Support for HM – CMC is hyperhonest and hyperdishonest (i.e. direct).

⊖ Types of CMC – theories ignore that disclosure varies in types of CMC.

⊖ CMC is multimodal – online/offline relationships occur together (complex).

Absence of gating

Easier to overcome obstacles (gates) online than FtF.

Can create different identity (e.g. less shy) or overcome barriers (e.g. stammer).

⊕ Research support – anxious people express 'true selves' more online (McKenna and Bargh).

Topic 2: RELATIONSHIPS

33

1 Self-disclosure happens less in CMC according to:
   (a) Hyperpersonal model.
   (b) Absence of gating.
   (c) Reduced cues theory.

2 According to the hyperpersonal model, online relationships:
   (a) Are by definition superficial.
   (b) Are better than face-to-face ones.
   (c) Start and end quickly.

3 There may be more disclosure in CMC than face-to-face because:
   (a) Emotions are easy to communicate.
   (b) Self-image can be manipulated.
   (c) Gating is greater.

4 In the context of CMC a 'gate' is:
   (a) Any obstacle to a relationship.
   (b) Always a positive thing.
   (c) A hinged barrier in a wall, usually metal or wood.

5 The cues in CMC are:
   (a) Better than face-to-face.
   (b) Different from face-to-face.
   (c) Less effective than face-to-face.

6 Hyperpersonal communication is:
   (a) Direct and intimate.
   (b) Evasive and superficial.
   (c) More common face-to-face than in CMC.

7 Theories of CMC fail to acknowledge that:
   (a) There are different types of CMC.
   (b) Face-to-face is best.
   (c) Virtual relationships are difficult.

8 When online, anxious people:
   (a) Fail to form relationships.
   (b) Face many 'gates'.
   (c) Can be their 'true selves'.

Answers
1C 2C 3B 4A
5B 6A 7A 8C

Possible extended writing questions:
- Discuss research into virtual relationships in social media. *[AL = 16]*
- Describe and evaluate self-disclosure in virtual relationships. *[AL = 8]*
- Outline and evaluate the effects of absence of gating on the nature of virtual relationships. *[AL = 8]*

Spec Spotlight

Parasocial relationships: levels of parasocial relationships, the absorption addiction model and the attachment theory explanation.

Levels theory

Maltby *et al.* – three levels of parasocial relationship (Celebrity Attitude Scale).

Entertainment-social (least intense), intense-personal, borderline pathological.

⊖ Methodological issues – most studies self-report and correlational (no cause).

Absorption addiction model

McCutcheon – parasocial relationships help person overcome life deficiencies.

Initial interest (absorption) in celebrity – later addiction requires increasing 'doses'.

⊕ Research support – poor body image in females with intense celebrity worship (Maltby *et al.*).

⊖ Lacks explanatory power – only describes parasocial relationships.

Attachment theory

Early attachment problems make later relationships difficult, so seek parasocial ones.

Insecure-resistant more drawn to parasocial relationships (no threat of rejection).

⊕ Cross-cultural support – similar attachment to Harry Potter across cultures (Schmid and Klimmt).

⊖ Lacks support – no difference between secure and insecure (McCutcheon *et al.*).

1 **Levels of parasocial relationship are measured with the:**
   (a) Fame Opinions Scale.
   (b) Superstar Beliefs Scale.
   (c) Celebrity Attitude Scale.

2 **The most intense level is:**
   (a) Borderline pathological.
   (b) Entertainment-social.
   (c) Intense-personal.

3 **The theory that you need more and more parasocial involvement is:**
   (a) Absorption addiction model.
   (b) Attachment theory.
   (c) Levels of involvement theory.

4 **The attachment type most linked to parasocial relationships is:**
   (a) Secure.
   (b) Insecure-avoidant.
   (c) Insecure-resistant.

5 **A methodological problem with most studies is:**
   (a) They are lab experiments.
   (b) They are based on self-reports.
   (c) They are highly controlled.

6 **Females who most intensely worship celebrities:**
   (a) Have a poor body image.
   (b) Have eating disorders.
   (c) Are mostly emotionally stable.

7 **'Lacks explanatory power' means the absorption-addiction model:**
   (a) Is extremely valid.
   (b) Can only describe parasocial relationships.
   (c) States why such relationships exist.

8 **Attachment theory has received support from:**
   (a) Lab experiments.
   (b) McCutcheon et al.'s study.
   (c) Cross-cultural studies.

Answers
1C 2A 3A 4C
5B 6A 7B 8C

Possible extended writing questions:
- Outline and evaluate research related to parasocial relationships. *[AL = 16]*
- Discuss the absorption addiction model **and one other** explanation of parasocial relationships. *[AL = 16]*

Topic 3: GENDER

Sex and gender

Sex – biologically determined (chromosomal, anatomical, hormonal).

Biological status – innate/nature.

Gender – the attitudes, behaviours and roles associated with being male or female.

Psychosocial status – nurture.

Gender identity disorder is when sex and gender do not correspond – biological sex does not reflect how a person feels inside.

Spec Spotlight

Sex and gender.
Sex-role stereotypes.

Sex-role stereotypes

Social expectations shared by a culture or group about how males and females should behave.

May or may not be valid – some expectations have some basis in reality, but many are incorrect and can lead to sexist and damaging attitudes.

Sex-role stereotypes in the media – men shown in autonomous and professional roles in TV ads, women in familial and domestic settings (Furnham and Farragher).

1 Sex refers to someone's:
(a) Social status.
(b) Biological status.
(c) Psychological status.

2 Sex is influenced by:
(a) Nature.
(b) Nurture.
(c) Free will.

3 Gender does *not* include:
(a) Social attitudes.
(b) Psychological roles.
(c) Hormonal influences.

4 This may happen when sex and gender do *not* correspond:
(a) Gender stability disorder.
(b) Gender constancy disorder.
(c) Gender identity disorder.

5 All sex-role stereotypes are:
(a) Based in reality.
(b) Incorrect.
(c) A mixture of valid and not valid.

6 Found evidence of sex-role stereotyping in TV ads.:
(a) Burnham and Carragher:
(b) Denham and Gallagher.
(c) Furnham and Farragher.

7 On TV, women more likely to be depicted in:
(a) Domestic settings.
(b) Professional roles.
(c) Positions of autonomy.

8 A social expectation shared by a culture or group:
(a) Stereophonic.
(b) Sellotape.
(c) Stereotype.

Answers
1B 2A 3C 4C
5C 6C 7A 8C

Possible extended writing questions:
- Distinguish between sex and gender. *[AL = 3]*
- Using an example, explain what is meant by a 'sex-role stereotype'. *[AL = 3]*

Androgyny and the BSRI

Spec Spotlight

Androgyny and
measuring androgyny,
including the Bem Sex
Role Inventory.

AO1

Defining androgyny

Balance of masculine and feminine traits, behaviours, attitudes.

Positive – high androgyny is associated with psychological well-being (Bem).

Measuring androgyny (BSRI)

Bem Sex Role Inventory – items are masculine (e.g. dominant), feminine (e.g. gentle) or neutral (e.g. friendly).

BSRI has 60 questions on a 7-point scale (20 M, 20 F, 20 N), 7 = always true.

Categorisation as masculine (high M, low F score) and as feminine (high F, low M).

Androgynous (high M, high F) and undifferentiated (low M, low F).

AO3

⊕ BSRI is reliable and valid – selected traits confirmed in follow-up studies.

⊖ Link between well-being and androgyny challenged – link due to better adjustment (Adams and Sherer).

⊖ Gender identity cannot be reduced to a single score – more global concept.

⊖ Lack of temporal and cultural validity of BSRI – outdated, stereotypical.

⊖ Questionnaires are subjective and biased – issue of social desirability.

1 A balance between masculine and feminine traits:
(a) Ambiguity.
(b) Antipathy.
(c) Androgyny.

2 Designed the Sex Role Inventory:
(a) Bem.
(b) Fem.
(c) Gem.

3 Number of items on the BSRI:
(a) 5
(b) 60
(c) 90

4 Associated with psychological well-being:
(a) High androgyny.
(b) Low androgyny.
(c) Undifferentiated.

5 Low masculine score, low feminine score:
(a) Undifferentiated.
(b) Androgyny.
(c) Neutral.

6 On the BSRI, questions are measured on a:
(a) 5-point-scale.
(b) 7-point-scale.
(c) 9-point-scale.

7 A problem with questionnaires:
(a) Social unreliability.
(b) Social specificity.
(c) Social desirability.

8 Challenged link between androgyny and well-being:
(a) Sutton and Sherer.
(b) Adams and Sherer.
(c) Alan and Sherer.

Answers
1C 2A 3B 4A
5A 6B 7C 8B

Possible extended writing questions:

- Discuss research related to androgyny. *[AL = 16]*
- Describe and evaluate Bem's Sex Role Inventory as a method of measuring androgyny. *[AL = 16]*

AO1

The role of chromosomes and hormones

AO3

The role of chromosomes

Chromosome 23 determines biological sex.

Y chromosome – female is XX, male is XY.
Y chromosome has SRY gene.

The role of hormones

Gender developments governed by hormones.

Testosterone – male development, aggressive behaviour.

Oestrogen – female development, menstruation, pre-menstrual syndrome (PMS) and emotionality.

Oxytocin – stimulates lactation, reduces cortisol, facilitates bonding (love hormone).

⊕ Research support – aggression linked to levels of testosterone, e.g. prison study (Dabbs *et al.*).

⊖ Contradictory evidence – testosterone/ placebo injection study (Tricker *et al.*).

⊖ PMS as a medical category is controversial – a social construction.

⊖ Overemphasis on nature – cannot explain cross-cultural differences.

⊖ Oversimplifies a complex concept – ignores thought and childhood conflict.

Topic 3: GENDER

Spec Spotlight

The role of chromosomes and hormones (testosterone, oestrogen and oxytocin) in sex and gender.

1 The chromosome that determines biological sex:

(a) 23

(b) 32

(c) 46

2 Male chromosomal pattern:

(a) XY.

(b) XX.

(c) XO.

3 Linked to aggressive behaviour:

(a) Oxytocin.

(b) Insulin.

(c) Testosterone.

4 Sometimes called the 'love hormone':

(a) Testosterone.

(b) Oestrogen.

(c) Oxytocin.

5 *Not* a function of oxytocin:

(a) Facilitates bonding.

(b) Increases cortisol.

(c) Stimulates lactation.

6 Conducted the testosterone injection study:

(a) Dabbs *et al.*

(b) Bem.

(c) Tricker *et al.*

7 Ignored by the biological model of gender:

(a) Influence of hormones.

(b) Influence of childhood conflict.

(c) Influence of genes.

8 Criticised by feminists as a social construction:

(a) Pre-menstrual syndrome.

(b) Post-menstrual syndrome.

(c) Pre-mens syndrome.

Answers

1A 2A 3C 4C

5B 6C 7A 8A

Possible extended writing questions:

- Discuss the role of chromosomes **and** hormones in gender. *[AL = 16]*
- Outline and evaluate the role of testosterone, oestrogen **and** oxytocin in gender. *[AL = 16]*

AO1

AO3

Topic 3: GENDER

Book-link

Y2/A Student Book
Pages 154–155

Y2/A Revision Guide
Pages 96–97

Spec Spotlight

Atypical sex
chromosome patterns:
Klinefelter's syndrome
and Turner's syndrome.

Klinefelter's syndrome

Anatomical male – additional X chromosome (XXY).

Physical – less body hair, some breast, small genitals, clumsiness, rounded body.

Psychological – poor language, passive, shy, easily stressed, poor problem solving.

Turner's syndrome

Anatomical female – absence of one X chromosome (XO).

Physical – infertility, shield chest, low-set ears, webbed neck, narrow hips.

Psychological – good language, poor visual memory, poor maths, socially immature.

⊕ Contribution to nature–nurture debate – differences have biological basis.

⊖ Lack of causal relationship – differences may be due to social factors.

⊕ Real-life application – identification and treatment from young age has benefits.

⊖ Unrepresentative, atypical samples – can't generalise to typical development.

⊖ 'Typical' sex and gender may have been exaggerated – more differences within than between sexes (Maccoby and Jacklin).

1 Chromosomal pattern of Klinefelter's individuals:
(a) XY.
(b) XXY.
(c) XO.

2 *Not* a physical characteristic of Klinefelter's:
(a) Small genitals.
(b) Clumsiness.
(c) Narrow hips.

3 A psychological characteristic of Klinefelter's:
(a) Passive.
(b) Good language ability.
(c) Overconfidence.

4 Chromosomal pattern of Turner's individuals:
(a) XO.
(b) XX.
(c) XYY.

5 A physical characteristic of Turner's:
(a) Fertility.
(b) High set ears.
(c) Webbed neck.

6 A psychological characteristic of Turner's:
(a) Good memory.
(b) Good maths ability
(c) Good language ability.

7 Found greater differences within genders than between:
(a) McCauley and Jackson.
(b) Maccoby and Jacklin.
(c) McClintock and Jackman.

8 *Not* a strength of research into atypical sex chromosomes:
(a) Real-life application.
(b) Contribution to nature–nurture debate.
(c) Established causal relationship.

Answers
1B 2C 3A 4A
5C 6C 7B 8C

Possible extended writing questions:

- Describe and evaluate research into atypical sex chromosome patterns. *[AL = 16]*
- Discuss research into Turner's syndrome **and/or** Klinefelter's syndrome. *[AL = 16]*

Cognitive explanations: Kohlberg's theory

Book-link

Y2/A Student Book
Pages 156–157

Y2/A Revision Guide
Pages 98–99

Spec Spotlight

Cognitive explanations of gender development, Kohlberg's theory, gender identity, gender stability and gender constancy.

AO1

Cognitive developmental – cognitive = thinking, developmental = changes over time.

Gender development parallels intellectual development, related to Piaget.

Stage 1: **Gender identity** (2 years) – can label own and others' gender.

Stage 2: **Gender stability** (4 years) – know their gender stays the same but can't apply to others.

Stage 3: **Gender constancy** (6 years) – know gender stays same across time and situations.

After constancy, children seek out gender-appropriate role models to imitate.

AO3

⊕ Research support – watched both males/females in identity stage but selective in constancy stage (Slaby and Frey).

⊕ Support from biological approach – cross-cultural evidence (Munroe *et al.*).

⊖ Gender-appropriate behaviour might begin earlier (Bussey and Bandura).

⊖ Validity of interviews is questionable – children cannot express thoughts.

⊖ Social learning theory challenges focus on maturation – boys less flexible.

1 The approximate age of Kohlberg's first stage:
(a) 2 years.
(b) 4 years.
(c) 6 years.

2 *Not* one of Kohlberg's stages of gender development:
(a) Gender identity.
(b) Gender stability.
(c) Gender complexity.

3 Understanding one's own gender stays the same but *not* others':
(a) Gender identity.
(b) Gender stability.
(c) Gender constancy.

4 At the third stage, children seek out role models to:
(a) Interpret.
(b) Imitate.
(c) Interview.

5 Kohlberg's theory is best described as:
(a) Cognitive-social.
(b) Cognitive-biological.
(c) Cognitive-developmental.

6 Found evidence of identification in the constancy stage:
(a) Stacy and Faith.
(b) Slaby and Frey.
(c) South and Fry.

7 Kohlberg's focus on maturation has been challenged by:
(a) Social learning theory.
(b) Psychodynamic theory.
(c) Biological theory.

8 Biological aspect of Kohlberg's theory supported by:
(a) Social learning theory.
(b) Cross-cultural evidence.
(c) Field studies.

Answers
1A 2C 3B 4B
5C 6B 7A 8B

Possible extended writing questions:
- Discuss **one** cognitive explanation of gender. [AL = 16]
- Describe and evaluate Kohlberg's theory of gender. [AL = 16]

Book-link

Y2/A Student Book
Pages 158–159

Y2/A Revision Guide
Pages 100–101

Spec Spotlight

Cognitive
explanations of
gender development,
gender schema theory.

A01   Cognitive explanations: Gender schema theory   A03

Understanding of gender changes with age (Martin and Halverson).

Gender schema – mental constructs contain and organise our knowledge of gender.

Gender schema after gender identity (2–3 years) – seek information to develop schema.

GST places search for gender-appropriate information earlier than Kohlberg suggested.

Gender-appropriate schema expand over time and direct child's behaviour.

Ingroup information is remembered better than outgroup information – by age 8 children have schema for both genders.

⊕ Research support – remember gender-consistent photographs (Martin and Halverson).

⊕ Can explain young children's rigid gender beliefs – ingroup schema.

⊕ Complements Kohlberg's theory – schema and constancy different (memory versus motivation).

⊖ Importance of schema has been exaggerated – overlooks social factors.

⊖ There may be no link – schema may not determine behaviour.

Topic 3: GENDER

1 Children develop schema when they achieve:
(a) Gender identity.
(b) Gender stability.
(c) Gender constancy.

2 GST predicts that children search for gender-appropriate information:
(a) Earlier than Kohlberg suggested.
(b) Later than Kohlberg suggested.
(c) At the same time.

3 According to GST, gender identity occurs between the ages of:
(a) 1 and 2.
(b) 2 and 3.
(c) 3 and 4.

4 Children best remember the gender behaviour of their:
(a) Outgroup.
(b) Ingroup.
(c) Peer group.

5 Gender-appropriate schema:
(a) Reduce over time.
(b) Expand over time.
(c) Stay the same.

6 Conducted study of gender-consistent photographs:
(a) Marvin and Helgerson.
(b) Merlin and Hartson.
(c) Martin and Halverson.

7 A strength of GST:
(a) Clear link between schema and behaviour.
(b) Theory incorporates social factors.
(c) Explains children's rigid beliefs.

8 Children develop detailed schema for both genders at age:
(a) 7
(b) 8
(c) 9

Answers
1A 2A 3B 4B
5B 6C 7C 8B

Possible extended writing questions:
- Discuss **two** cognitive explanations of gender. *[AL = 16]*
- Outline and evaluate gender schema theory. *[AL = 16]*

Book-link

Y2/A Student Book
Pages 160–161

Y2/A Revision Guide
Pages 102–103

Spec Spotlight

Psychodynamic explanation of gender development, Freud's psychoanalytic theory, Oedipus complex, Electra complex; identification and internalisation.

AO1

Phallic stage (age 3–6 years) – key time for gender, pre-phallic children are bisexual.

Oedipus complex in boys – feelings for mother, jealous of father, fear castration.

Electra complex in girls – penis envy, in competition with mother, resentment too.

Resolution – both resolved through identification with same-sex parent.

Identification leads to **internalisation** of parents' identity, adopt attitudes and values.

Little Hans – Oedipus complex, fear of horses was displaced fear of castration.

AO3

⊖ Lack of support for Oedipus complex – boys with liberal fathers more masculine (Blakemore).

⊖ Theory doesn't explain female development – men have womb envy (Horney).

⊖ Children with different gender parents – normal development (Golombok et al.).

⊖ Freud's methods lack scientific rigour – untestable pseudoscience.

⊖ Conflicts with other gender theories – process more complex and gradual than Freud's version.

Topic 3: GENDER

49

1 Pre-phallic children are:
  (a) Homosexual.
  (b) Asexual.
  (c) Bisexual.

2 Between 3 and 6 years of age is the:
  (a) Oral stage.
  (b) Phallic stage.
  (c) Latency stage.

3 Boys experience incestuous feelings and fear castration:
  (a) The Electra complex.
  (b) The Oedipus complex.
  (c) The Psychosexual complex.

4 Gender identity comes about through:
  (a) Identification and internalisation.
  (b) Imitation and initiation.
  (c) Invitation and illustration.

5 Little Hans developed a fear of horses through:
  (a) Replacement.
  (b) Misplacement.
  (c) Displacement.

6 According to Horney, males experience:
  (a) Ovary envy.
  (b) Womb envy.
  (c) Penis envy.

7 Who found a lack of support for the Oedipus complex?
  (a) Blackmore.
  (b) Blackwell.
  (c) Blakemore.

8 In contrast to Freud's theory, other theories suggest gender is a:
  (a) Quicker process.
  (b) More gradual process.
  (c) Less complex process.

Topic 3: GENDER

Answers
1C 2B 3B 4A
5C 6B 7C 8B

Possible extended writing questions:
- Discuss **one** psychodynamic explanation of gender development. *[AL = 16]*
- Describe and evaluate Freud's psychoanalytic theory of gender development. *[AL = 16]*

Social learning explanation of gender development

A01

A03

A01

Gender is learned by observation and reinforcement – in a social context.

Gender-appropriate behaviours – differentially reinforced in boys and girls.

Vicarious reinforcement and punishment – influences imitation of gender behaviour.

Children identify with role models – e.g. parents, teachers, attractive, same sex.

Gender behaviour is modelled and then imitated – e.g. copy mother's cooking.

Mediational processes – attention, retention, motivation, motor reproduction.

A03

⊕ Research support for differential reinforcement – babies dressed as boys or girls (Smith and Lloyd).

⊕ SLT can explain changing gender roles in society – different reinforcements.

⊖ SLT doesn't explain developmental process – reinforcement same at any age.

⊖ SLT does not fully consider biological factors, e.g. the case of David Reimer.

⊖ SLT can't explain unconscious influences on gender development – meditational processes are conscious.

Spec Spotlight

Social learning theory as applied to gender development.

Social learning explanation of gender development – multiple choice questions

1 *Not* a feature of the social learning explanation of gender:
- (a) Unconscious conflict.
- (b) Imitation.
- (c) Observation.

2 The process of displaying a behaviour to be imitated:
- (a) Moulding.
- (b) Modelling.
- (c) Mastering.

3 Rewarding different behaviour in boys and girls is called:
- (a) Differential reinforcement.
- (b) Vicarious reinforcement.
- (c) Negative reinforcement.

4 *Not* a mediational process in learning gender:
- (a) Reaction.
- (b) Retention.
- (c) Attention.

5 Concept common to SLT and psychoanalytic theory:
- (a) Internalisation.
- (b) Imitation.
- (c) Identification.

6 Vicarious reinforcement refers to:
- (a) Direct rewards.
- (b) Indirect punishments.
- (c) Indirect rewards.

7 SLT does *not* fully consider biological factors such as:
- (a) The case of Donald Reagan.
- (b) The case of David Reimer.
- (c) The case of Daniel Richards.

8 Found support for differential reinforcement:
- (a) Smith and Jones.
- (b) Smith and Lloyd.
- (c) Smith and Turner.

Answers
1A 2B 3A 4A
5C 6C 7B 8B

Topic 3: GENDER

Possible extended writing questions:
- Outline and evaluate the social learning explanation of gender development. *[AL = 16]*
- Discuss **one or more** explanations of gender development. *[AL = 16]*

Book-link

Y2/A Student Book
Pages 164–165

Y2/A Revision Guide
Pages 106–107

Spec Spotlight

The influence of
culture and media
on gender roles.

The influence of culture and media on gender roles

AO1

Culture

Behaviour consistent across cultures = nature,
culturally specific = nurture.

Nurture: Mead – New Guinea tribes (Arapesh,
Mundugumor, Tchambuli) differed, suggests
gender culturally determined.

Nature: Buss – consistent mate preferences in
37 cultures.

Media

Children likely to imitate same-sex role models
who are reinforced.

Media creates gender stereotypes – men
autonomous, women domestic.

Positive correlation – more exposure to media,
more stereotypical behaviour.

AO3

⊖ Mead's findings challenged – biased and
misled participants (Freeman).

⊖ Imposed etic affects validity –
Western methods to study behaviour.

⊖ Research does not resolve nature–nurture
debate – cannot separate.

⊖ Research on the media is correlational –
cannot assume causation.

⊖ Counter-stereotypes also exist in the
media – positive effect (Pingree).

1 If behaviour is consistent across cultures, this supports:
(a) Nature.
(b) Nurture.
(c) An interactionist approach.

2 Where Mead's research was conducted:
(a) New Guinea.
(b) Western Samoa.
(c) New Zealand.

3 *Not* a tribe studied by Mead:
(a) Arapesh.
(b) Tchambuli.
(c) Leilani.

4 Relationship between media exposure and stereotyping:
(a) Negative.
(b) Positive.
(c) Zero.

5 *Not* a female gender stereotype:
(a) Dependent.
(b) Familial role.
(c) Autonomous.

6 Number of cultures studied by Buss:
(a) 35
(b) 37
(c) 39

7 Found counter-stereotypes in media could have positive effect:
(a) Pertwee.
(b) Pettigrew.
(c) Pingree.

8 Western researchers impose methods and understanding:
(a) Imposed etic.
(b) Imposed emic.
(c) Imposed exit.

Answers
1A 2A 3C 4B
5C 6B 7C 8A

Possible extended writing questions:
- Describe and evaluate the influence of culture **and** media on gender roles. *[AL = 16]*
- Briefly discuss the influence of culture **or** media on gender roles. *[AL = 8]*

Book-link

Y2/A Student Book
Pages 166–167

Y2/A Revision Guide
Pages 108–109

Spec Spotlight

Atypical gender
development: gender
identity disorder;
biological and social
explanations for gender
identity disorder.

A01

Gender identity disorder (GID) – mismatch between biological sex and gender.

Psychological disorder in DSM-5 – excludes biological conditions, e.g. Klinefelter's.

Biological explanations

Brain sex theory – BSTc 40% larger in males, reversed in transgender cases.

Genetic evidence – twin studies show 39% of cases were concordant (Heylens *et al.*).

Social explanations

Psychoanalytic theory – male GID extreme separation anxiety, symbiotic fusion.

Cognitive theory – counter-stereotypical activities create androgynous schema.

A03

⊖ Brain sex theory criticised – hormone therapy may change BSTc (Hulshoff Pol *et al.*).

⊖ Twin study evidence weak – low concordance, small samples.

⊖ Biological explanations oversimplify GID – reduced to genetic, hormonal level.

⊖ Psychoanalytic lacks support – absence of father has more effect in GID (Rekers).

⊖ Cognitive lacks explanatory power – how do non sex-typed schema develop?

Topic 3: GENDER

1 GID is a mismatch between gender and:
(a) Hormones.
(b) Biological sex.
(c) Chromosomes.

2 How much larger is the BSTc in males?
(a) 4%
(b) 14%
(c) 40%

3 GID is a psychological disorder in:
(a) MSD 5.
(b) DSM 5.
(c) SDM 5.

4 Psychoanalytic theory explains GID through a:
(a) Symbiotic fusion.
(b) Symbolic friction.
(c) Sympathetic frisson.

5 Concordance for MZ twins in Heylens *et al.* study:
(a) 33%
(b) 36%
(c) 39%

6 Found evidence against brain sex theory:
(a) Hulshoff Pol *et al.*
(b) Rekers Pol *et al.*
(c) Pol Thomas *et al.*

7 *Not* a criticism of twin studies:
(a) Small samples.
(b) High concordance.
(c) Environment is confounding.

8 *Not* a biological explanation of GID:
(a) Separation anxiety.
(b) Neuroanatomical basis.
(c) Hormonal influence.

Answers
1B 2C 3B 4A
5C 6A 7B 8A

Possible extended writing questions:

- Discuss research into atypical gender development. *[AL = 16]*
- Discuss biological and social explanations for gender identity disorder. *[AL = 16]*
- Outline and evaluate biological **or** social explanations for gender identity disorder. *[AL = 16]*

AO1 **AO3**

Book-link

Y2/A Student Book
Pages 178–179

Y2/A Revision Guide
Pages 110–111

Spec Spotlight

Piaget's theory of
cognitive development:
schemas, assimilation,
accommodation,
equilibration.

Maturation – causes changes in the way
children think.

Schema – units of knowledge which become
more abstract as we get older.

Disequilibrium – creates the motivation to
learn and explore.

Equilibration – a state of balance when
experience and current schema match.

Assimilation – new experience is incorporated
into existing schema.

Accommodation – creating new schema and
changing existing ones.

⊕ Supporting evidence – children learn by
forming mental representations (Howe
et al.).

⊕ Piaget's ideas revolutionised learning –
activity-oriented classrooms.

⊖ Piaget underestimated the role of other
people, unlike Vygotsky.

⊕ Role of equilibrium overemphasised –
studied middle-class children, more
motivated.

⊖ Full role of language – not acknowledged,
unlike Vygotsky.

Topic 4: COGNITION AND DEVELOPMENT

57

1 As we get older, schema become more:
(a) Abstract.
(b) Basic.
(c) Ambiguous.

2 Creates the motivation to learn and explore:
(a) Disinhibition.
(b) Disassociation.
(c) Disequilibrium.

3 When experience and current schema match:
(a) Assimilation.
(b) Equilibration.
(c) Accommodation.

4 New experience is incorporated into existing schema:
(a) Assimilation.
(b) Equilibration.
(c) Accommodation.

5 Creating new schema and changing existing ones:
(a) Assimilation.
(b) Equilibration.
(c) Accommodation.

6 Found evidence that children form mental representations:
(a) Lowe et al.
(b) Snow et al.
(c) Howe et al.

7 Piaget's ideas have been applied to:
(a) Education.
(b) Social work.
(c) The legal system.

8 Unlike Vygotsky, Piaget did not acknowledge the full role of:
(a) Maturation.
(b) Language.
(c) Cognition.

Answers
1A 2C 3B 4A
5C 6C 7A 8B

Possible extended writing questions:
- Discuss Piaget's theory of cognitive development. *[AL = 16]*
- Discuss how children learn according to Piaget. Refer to assimilation, accommodation **and** equilibration in your answer. *[AL = 16]*

Piaget's stages of intellectual development

Book-link

Y2/A Student Book
Pages 180–181

Y2/A Revision Guide
Pages 112–113

Spec Spotlight

Piaget's theory of cognitive development: stages of intellectual development. Characteristics of these stages including object permanence, conservation, egocentrism and class inclusion.

AO1

Children progress through four stages each with a different level of reasoning.

Stage 1: Sensorimotor stage (0–2 years) – includes **object permanence**.

Stage 2: Pre-operational stage (2–7) – includes **egocentrism** (three mountains task).

Lack of **class inclusion** – classifications have subsets, e.g. five dogs, two cats – more dogs than animals?

Stage 3: Concrete operations stage (7–11) – includes **conservation** (pouring water between beakers).

Stage 4: Formal operations stage (11+) – includes syllogisms and abstract reasoning.

AO3

⊖ Lack of validity – underestimated child's cognitive abilities, e.g. conservation (McGarrigle and Donaldson).

⊖ Lack of class inclusion – 5-year-olds OK with feedback (Siegler and Svetina).

⊖ Lack of egocentrism – not supported in policeman study (Hughes).

⊖ Children's abilities both under- and over-estimated – e.g. formal operations.

⊖ Intellectual development – evidence from studies of children with ASD that it is domain specific not domain general.

1 Piaget proposed _____ stages of intellectual development.
(a) Four.
(b) Five.
(c) Six.

2 The main task of the sensorimotor stage is to develop:
(a) Object permanence.
(b) Class inclusion.
(c) Abstract reasoning.

3 Egocentrism was testing using the:
(a) Three peaks task.
(b) Three-sided shape task.
(c) Three mountains task.

4 The concrete operations stage last from:
(a) 2–7 years.
(b) 7–11 years.
(c) 11–15 years.

5 Develops in formal operations:
(a) Soliloquies.
(b) Syllogisms.
(c) Simulations.

6 Hughes criticised egocentrism using the:
(a) Policemen study.
(b) Fireman study.
(c) Pilot study.

7 Piaget may have:
(a) Underestimated children's ability.
(b) Overestimated children's ability.
(c) Both.

8 Domain specific intelligence demonstrated in children who have:
(a) ADS.
(b) ASD.
(c) DSA.

Answers
1A 2A 3C 4B
5B 6A 7C 8B

Possible extended writing questions:

- Outline and evaluate Piaget's stages of intellectual development. *[AL = 16]*
- Discuss research into conservation, egocentrism **and** class inclusion. *[AL = 16]*

Book-link

Y2/A Student Book
Pages 182–183

Y2/A Revision Guide
Pages 114–115

Spec Spotlight

Vygotsky's theory of cognitive development, including the zone of proximal development and scaffolding.

AO1

Social processes – first intermental (between people), then intramental.

Cultural differences in learning – explained through differing experiences.

Zone of proximal development (ZPD)

Gap between current and potential abilities.

Increased skills and reasoning ability – help of experts, not just exploration.

Scaffolding

Experts help learner cross ZPD – recruitment, reduction in degrees of freedom, direction maintenance.

Progressive strategies – identified by Wood et al. from most to least help.

AO3

⊕ Evidence for the ZPD – children perform better with peers (Roazzi and Bryant).

⊕ Support for scaffolding – mothers used less intervention with older children (Conner and Cross).

⊕ Real-life application – peer tutoring in education (Van Keer and Verhaeghe).

⊖ Not all children the same – interaction doesn't produce same result (Howe et al.).

⊖ Individual differences – not all are acknowledged, e.g. personality.

Topic 4: COGNITION AND DEVELOPMENT

1 *Not* a form of knowledge proposed by Vygotsky:
(a) Incidental.
(b) Intermental.
(c) Intramental.

2 The gap between current and potential abilities:
(a) Zone of progressive development.
(b) Zone of proactive development.
(c) Zone of proximal development.

3 Helps the learner cross the ZPD:
(a) Scheduling.
(b) Scaffolding.
(c) Supporting.

4 Proposed progressive strategies to scaffold learning:
(a) Wood *et al.*
(b) Black *et al.*
(c) Lyons *et al.*

5 Found evidence that children perform better with peers:
(a) Rossini and Berger.
(b) Richie and Bruner.
(c) Roazzi and Bryant.

6 A practical application of Vygotsky's ideas:
(a) Peer pressure.
(b) Peer tutoring.
(c) Peer approval.

7 *Not* all individual differences are acknowledged, for example:
(a) Experiences.
(b) Personality.
(c) Genetics.

8 Increased skills come from the help of:
(a) Novices.
(b) Experts.
(c) Amateurs.

Answers
1A 2C 3B 4A
5C 6B 7B 8B

Possible extended writing questions:
- Discuss Vygotsky's theory of cognitive development. *[AL = 16]*
- Discuss the role of scaffolding **and** the zone of proximal development in learning. *[AL = 16]*

Baillargeon's explanation of infant abilities

Book-link

Y2/A Student Book
Pages 184–185

Y2/A Revision Guide
Pages 116–117

Spec Spotlight

Baillargeon's explanation of early infant abilities, including knowledge of the physical world; violation of expectation research.

AO1

Object permanence – inability may be due to poor motor skills, Baillargeon suggested more advanced abilities.

Knowledge of the physical world – innate *physical reasoning system* (PRS), gives infant abilities.

PRS – infants predisposed to attend and learn from impossible events.

Key study: Baillargeon and Graber

Procedure – **violation of expectation research**, short-tall rabbit study.

Findings – older infants looked longer, object permanence at 5–6 months.

AO3

⊕ VOE technique better – in Piaget's studies infants may have lost interest.

⊖ Hard to judge infant understanding – questions validity of VOE.

⊕ PRS explains universal behaviour – e.g. dropped object lands on floor (Hespos and van Marle).

⊖ VOE assumes behaviour indicates understanding – Piaget was looking at principles.

⊕ Findings consistent with research on other abilities – e.g. Pei *et al.* on distance perception.

Baillargeon's explanation of infant abilities – multiple choice questions

1 Baillargeon thought object permanence was due to:
(a) Poor cognitive development.
(b) Poor motor skills.
(c) Poor social skills.

2 VOE research stands for:
(a) Verification of evidence.
(b) Violation of expectation.
(c) Verdict of experience.

3 PRS stands for:
(a) Physical reasoning system.
(b) Personal reasoning system.
(c) Physical response system.

4 Using VOE to test infant abilities means you:
(a) Demonstrate physical abilities.
(b) Can be certain about infant understanding.
(c) Make inferences about cognitive abilities.

5 The Baillargeon and Graber study suggests object permanence develops:
(a) Earlier than Piaget suggested.
(b) Later than Piaget suggested.
(c) At about the same time as Piaget suggested.

6 The impossible event involved a:
(a) Short and tall rabbit.
(b) Big and small bear.
(c) Naughty teddy.

7 Difficulty judging what an infant understands is a problem of:
(a) Reliability.
(b) Reductionism.
(c) Validity.

8 The reason infants didn't display object permanence may be because:
(a) The study was done a long time ago.
(b) They were from middle-class families.
(c) They lost interest.

Topic 4: COGNITION AND DEVELOPMENT

Answers
1B 2B 3A 4C
5A 6A 7C 8C

Possible extended writing questions:
- Discuss Baillargeon's explanation of infant abilities. *[AL = 16]*
- Compare Baillargeon's **and** Piaget's explanation of infant abilities. *[AL = 16]*

Book-link

Y2/A Student Book
Pages 186–187

Y2/A Revision Guide
Pages 118–119

Spec Spotlight

The development of social cognition: Selman's levels of perspective-taking.

AO1 | **Social cognition: Selman's levels of perspective-taking** | **AO3**

Social perspective-taking – domain-specific (Selman) versus domain-general (Piaget).

Perspective-taking (PT) scenarios – e.g. Holly climbing trees to rescue kitten.

Stage theory – begins with social egocentrism (3–6 years).

Progressively see another person's perspective – five stages in total.

Stage 4 (12+ years) – social conventions needed to keep order.

Three further elements – fully explain social development, e.g. interpersonal understanding and negotiation strategies.

⊕ Research evidence – PT and age correlated in longitudinal study (Gurucharri and Selman).

⊖ Importance of PT – challenged, e.g. bullies showed PT (Gasser and Keller).

⊕ Atypical development – e.g. ADHD did worse on PT tasks (Manton *et al.*).

⊖ Only one aspect of social development – oversimplified account.

⊕ PT is learned – Chinese did better than US, cultural inputs (Wu and Keyser).

66

1 Selman argues that social perspective-taking is:
(a) Domain-general.
(b) Domain-specific.
(c) Domain-neutral.

2 A scenario used to investigate perspective-taking:
(a) Millie playing on the swings.
(b) Lily going on a picnic.
(c) Holly climbing trees.

3 Selman's stage theory begins with:
(a) Egocentrism.
(b) Class inclusion.
(c) Object permanence.

4 Stage 4 focuses on:
(a) Social interaction.
(b) Social convention.
(c) Social inhibition.

5 Number of stages in total:
(a) Three.
(b) Four.
(c) Five.

6 Selman identified further elements of social development including:
(a) Interpersonal understanding.
(b) Interpersonal strategies.
(c) Gender understanding.

7 The theory helps understanding of:
(a) PTSD.
(b) APD.
(c) ADHD.

8 Found support for perspective-taking being learned through experience:
(a) Zsu and Geisler.
(b) Wu and Keyser.
(c) Lou and Seizler.

Answers
1B 2C 3A 4B
5C 6A 7C 8B

Topic 4: COGNITION AND DEVELOPMENT

Possible extended writing questions:
- Discuss Selman's levels of perspective-taking. *[AL = 16]*
- Outline and evaluate **one** theory of the development of social cognition. *[AL = 16]*

Social cognition: Theory of mind (ToM)

Book-link

Y2/A Student Book
Pages 188–189

Y2/A Revision Guide
Pages 120–121

Spec Spotlight

The development of social cognition: theory of mind, including theory of mind as an explanation for autism; the Sally–Anne study.

AO1

Mind-reading – personal 'theory', knowing what other people know.

ToM test – toddlers watch adults put beads in a jar, imitated intentions (Meltzoff).

False belief task – Maxi and chocolate in blue cupboard (Wimmer and Perner).

Sally–Anne study – Anne hides marble, where does child think Sally looks for her marble?

Autistic spectrum disorder (ASD) – 20% showed lack of ToM compared to 85% controls (Baron-Cohen *et al.*).

Eyes Task – adults with high functioning ASD struggled (Baron-Cohen *et al.*).

AO3

⊖ Low validity of false belief tasks – require other cognitive abilities.

⊖ Difficult to distinguish ToM from perspective-taking – useless concept.

⊕ Application to understanding ASD – but may be only a partial explanation.

⊖ ToM development – preferable to understand whether nature or nurture.

⊖ Low validity of Eyes Task – static, different from real-life.

1 ToM has been described as the ability to:
   (a) Mind-read.
   (b) Brain scan.
   (c) Socially interact.

2 *Not* a way of testing ToM:
   (a) False-belief task.
   (b) Impossible figure task.
   (c) Beads in a jar task.

3 In the Sally–Anne task, who moves the marble to the box?
   (a) Sally.
   (b) Anne.
   (c) Tom.

4 Number of ASD children who succeed on the Sally-Anne task:
   (a) 85%
   (b) 5%
   (c) 20%

5 The Eyes Task was developed by:
   (a) Baron-Cohen *et al*.
   (b) Brown-Coburn *et al*.
   (c) Burns-Clarkson *et al*.

6 In the Sally–Anne task, a person with ToM thinks:
   (a) Sally will say basket.
   (b) Sally will say box.
   (c) Anne will say marble.

7 ToM has been applied to the understanding of:
   (a) ADHD.
   (b) APD.
   (c) ASD.

8 An example of a false belief task:
   (a) Maxi and the chocolate.
   (b) Patsy and the birthday cake.
   (c) Taxi and the motorway.

Answers
1A 2B 3B 4C
5A 6A 7C 8A

Possible extended writing questions:

- Discuss the theory of mind as an explanation of social cognition. *[AL = 16]*
- Describe and evaluate ways of investigating the theory of mind. *[AL = 16]*

Book-link

Y2/A Student Book
Pages 190–191

Y2/A Revision Guide
Pages 122–123

Spec Spotlight

The development of
social cognition:
The role of the mirror
neuron system in
social cognition.

Mirror neurons (MNs) – respond to motor
activity of others, first observed in monkeys.

MNs respond to intentions of others – not just
observed actions (Gallese and Goldman).

MNs involved in perspective-taking and the
development of ToM.

MNs key to human social evolution – for living
in large groups (Ramachandran).

ASD – lack perspective-taking skills, poor MN
system.

'Broken mirror' – prevents ASD children
imitating and understanding others.

⊕ Research support – Brodmann's area 9
involved in yawning (Haker *et al.*).

⊖ Difficult studying MNs in humans –
individual cells not measured.

⊖ Mixed evidence for the link with ASD –
not all findings have been replicated.

⊖ Inability to isolate specialist cells – some
question their existence (Hickok).

⊖ Link with social cognition – may be using
others' behaviour to plan our own.

1 Activation of mirror neurons first observed in:
(a) Rats.
(b) Monkeys.
(c) Mice.

2 As well as motor actions, mirror neurons help us respond to:
(a) Expectations.
(b) Inhibitions.
(c) Intentions.

3 Mirror neurons may play a role in the development of:
(a) Theory of brain.
(b) Theory of thought.
(c) Theory of mind.

4 Theory that links ASD to mirror neurons:
(a) Cracked mirror.
(b) Smashed mirror.
(c) Broken mirror.

5 Haker *et al.* found support for mirror neurons by studying:
(a) Yawning.
(b) Coughing.
(c) Sneezing.

6 Researcher who questioned the existence of mirror neurons:
(a) Haycock.
(b) Hickok.
(c) Hiccup.

7 Mirror neurons are thought to play a role in:
(a) Perception-making.
(b) Impression formation.
(c) Perspective-taking.

8 Mirror neurons help us live in large groups as part of:
(a) Social evolution.
(b) Social devolution.
(c) Social revolution.

Answers
1B 2C 3C 4C
5A 6B 7C 8A

Possible extended writing questions:

- Discuss the role of the mirror neuron system in social cognition. *[AL = 16]*
- Describe and evaluate research into mirror neurons. *[AL = 16]*

Diagnosis and classification of schizophrenia

Book-link

Y2/A Student Book
Page 202–203

Y2/A Revision Guide
Pages 124–125

Spec Spotlight

Classification of schizophrenia. Positive symptoms of schizophrenia, including hallucinations and delusions. Negative symptoms of schizophrenia, including speech poverty and avolition. Reliability and validity in diagnosis and classification of schizophrenia, including reference to co-morbidity, culture and gender bias and symptom overlap.

71

AO1

Classification differs – DSM-5 (one positive symptom), ICD-10 (two negative symptoms).

Positive symptoms

Hallucinations – distorted experiences of reality.

Delusions – beliefs with no basis in reality, lead to 'bizarre' behaviour.

Negative symptoms

Avolition – severe loss of motivation, low activity levels.

Speech poverty – reduced amount and quality of speech (e.g. disorganised).

Reliability and validity in diagnosis and classification

Threatened by co-morbidity, symptom overlap.

AO3

⊖ Low **reliability** – little agreement between psychiatrists (Cheniaux *et al.*).

⊖ Low **validity** – schizophrenia more likely diagnosed using ICD than DSM.

⊖ **Co-morbidity/system overlap** – schizophrenia often occurs with other disorders, e.g. depression, reduces validity.

⊖ **Gender bias** – men more likely diagnosed, women function better.

⊖ **Culture bias** – Americans/British of African origin more likely diagnosed.

1 DSM-5 requires _____ for a diagnosis of schizophrenia.
(a) One positive and one negative symptom.
(b) Two negative symptoms.
(c) One positive symptom.

2 A positive symptom of schizophrenia is:
(a) Speech poverty.
(b) Delusions.
(c) Avolition.

3 Experiencing distortions of reality is what kind of symptom?
(a) Non-existent.
(b) Negative.
(c) Positive.

4 An example of speech poverty is:
(a) Producing lots of words.
(b) Disorganised sentences.
(c) Fluent language with no pauses.

5 When psychiatrists disagree over diagnosis of the same symptoms:
(a) Reliability is low.
(b) Co-morbidity is low.
(c) Validity is high.

6 Co-morbidity refers to:
(a) Fear of death.
(b) Negative symptoms of schizophrenia.
(c) Two disorders being diagnosed at the same time.

7 Less likely to be diagnosed with schizophrenia:
(a) Women.
(b) Men.
(c) Teenage boys.

8 Americans and British people of African origin are:
(a) More likely to be diagnosed with schizophrenia.
(b) Less likely to be diagnosed with schizophrenia.
(c) Never diagnosed with schizophrenia.

Topic 5: SCHIZOPHRENIA

Answers
1C 2B 3C 4B
5A 6C 7A 8A

Possible extended writing questions:
- Outline positive **and** negative symptoms of schizophrenia. *[AL = 6]*
- Discuss reliability **and** validity in the diagnosis and classification of schizophrenia. *[AL = 16]*

AO1 **AO3**

Book-link

Y2/A Student Book
Page 204–205

Y2/A Revision Guide
Pages 126–127

Spec Spotlight

Biological
explanations for
schizophrenia:
genetics, the
dopamine hypothesis
and neural
correlates.

Genetics

Runs in families – MZ twins 48% concordance versus DZ twins 17% (Gottesman).

Polygenic (many genes) and aetiologically heterogeneous (different combinations of genes).

Dopamine hypothesis

High activity linked to subcortex and hallucinations.

Low activity – associated with prefrontal cortex and disorders of thought.

Neural correlates

Avolition linked with low activity in ventral striatum.

Hallucinations – linked with low activity in superior temporal gyrus.

(+) Genetic vulnerability – adopted children of schizophrenics at greater risk (Tienari *et al.*).

(−) Mixed support – role for dopamine but also other transmitters (e.g. glutamate).

(−) Correlation versus causation – unusual brain activity may not cause schizophrenia.

(+) Role of mutation – link with paternal age (Brown *et al.*).

(−) Environment involved – interactionist approach: biological and psychological.

1 Kind of twins that have greater risk for schizophrenia:
   (a) BZ twins.
   (b) DZ twins.
   (c) MZ twins.

2 The role of genes in schizophrenia is currently best described as:
   (a) Polygenic.
   (b) One gene is mainly responsible.
   (c) Minimal.

3 Hallucinations are associated with:
   (a) Low dopamine activity.
   (b) High dopamine activity.
   (c) The prefrontal cortex.

4 Avolition has been linked with:
   (a) High ventral striatum activity.
   (b) High superior temporal gyrus activity.
   (c) Low ventral striatum activity.

5 The strongest evidence for genetic vulnerability comes from:
   (a) Laboratory experiments.
   (b) Adoption studies.
   (c) Questionnaire studies.

6 There is a strong link between schizophrenia and:
   (a) Paternal age.
   (b) Maternal age.
   (c) Serotonin.

7 Another neurotransmitter involved in schizophrenia is:
   (a) Adrenaline.
   (b) Glutamate.
   (c) GABA.

8 Unusual brain activity _____ schizophrenia.
   (a) Almost certainly causes.
   (b) Has no link to.
   (c) Is only correlated with.

Answers
1C 2A 3B 4C
5B 6A 7B 8C

Possible extended writing questions:

- Discuss **two** biological explanations for schizophrenia. *[AL = 16]*
- Outline and evaluate the roles of genetics **and** dopamine in explaining schizophrenia. *[AL = 16]*

Book-link

Y2/A Student Book
Page 206–207

Y2/A Revision Guide
Pages 128–129

AO1 — **AO3**

Topic 5: SCHIZOPHRENIA

Family dysfunction

Created by schizophrenogenic mothers (cold, rejecting).

Double-binds – trapped in confusing family communication (no way to get it right).

Expressed emotion – family criticism and hostility lead to relapse in patients.

$\ominus$ Retrospective research – memories of childhood experiences inaccurate.

$\ominus$ Weak evidence – based mostly on clinical observations (interpretations).

Spec Spotlight

Psychological explanations for schizophrenia: family dysfunction and cognitive explanations, including dysfunctional thought processing.

Cognitive explanations

Dysfunctional thought processing (in areas of brain), e.g. ventral striatum.

Dysfunction of metarepresentation – cannot recognise thoughts as one's own.

Central control dysfunction – cannot suppress automatic responses, leads to speech poverty.

$\oplus$ Research support – differences in patients (e.g. central control dysfunctions).

$\ominus$ Overlooks other factors – such as biological (e.g. genetics), both interact.

$\ominus$ Causality – unclear if cognitive factors are cause or effect of neural factors.

1 Schizophrenogenic mothers are:
(a) Loving and caring.
(b) Cold and rejecting.
(c) Laid back and happy.

2 A form of family communication that traps the schizophrenic is:
(a) Double-bind.
(b) Double-blind.
(c) Double-mind.

3 Inability to recognise one's own thoughts is a dysfunction of:
(a) Representation.
(b) Metarepresentation.
(c) Presentation.

4 Dysfunction of central control leads to:
(a) Speech poverty.
(b) Hallucinations.
(c) Avolition.

5 Family relationships research is limited because it is often:
(a) Prospective.
(b) Retrospective.
(c) Laboratory-based.

6 Clinical observations are:
(a) Highly reliable.
(b) Easy to validate.
(c) Open to interpretation.

7 Psychological factors _____ biological factors.
(a) Are more important than.
(b) Interact with.
(c) Are irrelevant compared with.

8 Cognitive impairments in schizophrenia:
(a) May cause neural dysfunction.
(b) May be caused by neural dysfunction.
(c) Both of the above.

Answers
1B 2A 3B 4A
5B 6C 7B 8C

Possible extended writing questions:
- Describe and evaluate **one or more** psychological explanations for schizophrenia. *[AL = 16]*
- Discuss **one** biological and **one** psychological explanation for schizophrenia. *[AL = 16]*

AO1

Biological therapies for schizophrenia: Drug therapy

AO3

Typical antipsychotics

Dopamine antagonists, reduce dopamine activity.

Block dopamine – *chlorpromazine* blocks receptors, normalises neurotransmission.

Sedative effect – *chlorpromazine* affects histamine receptors, has calming effect.

Atypical antipsychotics

Target range of neurotransmitters, minimise side effects.

Clozapine – binds to dopamine, glutamate and serotonin receptors.

Risperidone – binds more strongly to dopamine than serotonin receptors.

$\oplus$ Research evidence – both types moderately more effective than placebo (e.g. Thornley *et al.*).

$\ominus$ Side effects – mild, serious and fatal (e.g. neuroleptic malignant syndrome).

$\ominus$ Theoretical objection – tied to dopamine hypothesis, may be invalid.

$\ominus$ True effectiveness? – benefits overestimated in research (Healy).

$\ominus$ 'Chemical cosh' – unethical, used to sedate and make patients manageable.

1 Typical antipsychotics:
(a) Reduce serotonin levels.
(b) Increase dopamine activity.
(c) Are dopamine antagonists.

2 The effect of *chlorpromazine* on patients is:
(a) Sedative.
(b) Stimulating.
(c) Neutral.

3 Atypical antipsychotics:
(a) Affect just dopamine receptors.
(b) Target several neurotransmitters.
(c) Affect just serotonin receptors.

4 *Risperidone* binds most strongly to:
(a) Dopamine receptors.
(b) Serotonin receptors.
(c) Glutamate receptors.

5 The best way to describe antipsychotics is:
(a) Extremely effective.
(b) Moderately better than placebo.
(c) Atypicals are much better than typicals.

6 The side effects of antipsychotics:
(a) Are nearly always mild.
(b) Are mostly serious.
(c) Range from mild to potentially fatal.

7 Healy argues that the benefits of antipsychotics are:
(a) Long term as well as short term.
(b) Exaggerated by research.
(c) Extremely positive.

8 Using antipsychotics as a 'chemical cosh':
(a) Is ethically unacceptable.
(b) Is practically unheard of.
(c) Makes patients hard to manage.

Answers
1C 2A 3B 4A
5B 6C 7B 8A

Possible extended writing questions:

- Outline and evaluate **one** biological therapy for schizophrenia. *[AL = 16]*
- Discuss drug therapy as a biological therapy for schizophrenia. Refer in your answer to **both** typical **and** atypical antipsychotics. *[AL = 16]*

Psychological therapies for schizophrenia

Topic 5: SCHIZOPHRENIA

Cognitive behaviour therapy (CBT)

CBT aims to identify and change irrational thoughts.

Helps patients understand symptoms – e.g. hearing voices is OK, reduces anxiety.

Family therapy

Reduce expressed emotion, improve communication.

Improve family functioning – by reducing anger (Pharoah *et al.*).

Token economies

Tokens reinforce 'good' behaviour (operant conditioning).

Secondary reinforcers – tokens associated with valued rewards.

⊖ Limited benefits – evidence shows therapies only moderately effective (Pharoah *et al.*).

⊖ No cure – therapies have some benefits (e.g. reduce stress) but are not cures.

⊖ Ethical issues – deny human rights and freedom of thought, discrimination.

⊖ Quality of evidence – many studies lack control group or random allocation.

⊖ 'Alternative' therapies – under-researched (e.g. art therapy), should be monitored.

Spec Spotlight

Cognitive behaviour therapy and family therapy as used in the treatment of schizophrenia. Token economies as used in the management of schizophrenia.

1 The main aim of CBT is to:
(a) Identify genetic vulnerabilities.
(b) Rebalance neurotransmitter levels.
(c) Change irrational thinking.

2 Reducing expressed emotion is the main aim of:
(a) Token economies.
(b) Family therapy.
(c) Drug therapy.

3 Pharoah et al. claim one way to improve family functioning is to:
(a) Limit communication.
(b) Reduce feelings of guilt.
(c) Ignore the schizophrenic's behaviour.

4 Tokens used in token economies are:
(a) Primary reinforcers.
(b) Conditioned responses.
(c) Secondary reinforcers.

5 The best way to describe psychological therapies is they:
(a) Offer only moderate benefits.
(b) Are extremely effective.
(c) Are next to useless.

6 Psychological therapies:
(a) Are a waste of time.
(b) Do not reduce symptoms.
(c) Do not cure schizophrenia.

7 Many studies of therapies:
(a) Lack a control group.
(b) Underestimate their effectiveness.
(c) Allocate participants randomly.

8 'Alternative' psychological therapies are:
(a) Under-researched.
(b) Very well understood.
(c) Highly effective.

Answers
1C 2B 3B 4C
5A 6C 7A 8A

Possible extended writing questions:
- Discuss **two or more** psychological therapies for schizophrenia. *[AL = 16]*
- Outline and evaluate token economies as used in the management of schizophrenia. *[AL = 16]*

Book-link

Y2/A Student Book
Page 212–213
Y2/A Revision Guide
Pages 134–135

Spec Spotlight

The importance of an interactionist approach in explaining and treating schizophrenia; the diathesis-stress model.

The interactionist approach to schizophrenia

AO1

Explanation: Diathesis-stress model

Vulnerability (diathesis) and stress (trigger) interact.

Meehl's model – 'schizogene' makes you vulnerable to effects of chronic stress.

Modern understanding of diathesis – not a single gene, may not even be genetic.

Modern understanding of stress – any potential trigger (e.g. cannabis use).

Treatment

Antipsychotic drugs plus CBT, biological/psychological interaction.

Interactionist treatment – combining CBT and drugs more common in UK than USA.

AO3

(+) Research support – adopted children, combined genetic risk and family stress (Tienari et al.).

(−) Too simplistic – original views of diathesis and stress outdated.

(+) Usefulness – interactionist treatments have superior outcomes for patients (Tarrier et al.).

(−) Not clear how it works – incomplete understanding of underlying mechanisms.

(−) Treatment-causation fallacy – superior treatment does not mean interactionist explanation is correct.

1 Schizophrenia is most likely caused by:
- (a) Genes.
- (b) A diathesis triggered by stress.
- (c) Environmental factors.

2 The modern view of a diathesis is that it is:
- (a) A single 'schizogene'.
- (b) An environmental stressor.
- (c) Not necessarily genetic.

3 A more effective treatment of schizophrenia is:
- (a) A combination of drugs and CBT.
- (b) Psychological therapies alone.
- (c) Biological therapies alone.

4 Interactionist treatment is:
- (a) More common in the UK than the USA.
- (b) More common in the USA than the UK.
- (c) Not used in the UK at all.

5 Schizophrenia is linked with genetic risk and family stress in Tienari *et al.*'s study of:
- (a) Adopted children.
- (b) Identical twins.
- (c) Non-identical twins.

6 Views of both diathesis and stress:
- (a) Have always been complex.
- (b) Are now more complex than they were.
- (c) Are currently quite simplistic.

7 The mechanisms combining diathesis and stress are:
- (a) Irrelevant to understanding schizophrenia.
- (b) Very well understood.
- (c) Currently unclear.

8 Interactionist treatment is effective, so the diathesis-stress model:
- (a) Is completely wrong.
- (b) Must be right.
- (c) Could be right.

Topic 5: SCHIZOPHRENIA

Answers
1B 2C 3A 4A
5A 6B 7C 8C

Possible extended writing questions:
- Outline and evaluate the importance of an interactionist approach in explaining **and/or** treating schizophrenia. *[AL = 16]*
- Discuss the diathesis-stress model in relation to explaining **and** treating schizophrenia. *[AL = 16]*

Book-link

Y2/A Student Book
Pages 224–225

Y2/A Revision Guide
Pages 136–137

Spec Spotlight

Explanations for
food preferences: the
evolutionary explanation,
including reference to
neophobia and taste
aversion.

AO1

Explanations for food preferences: Evolutionary

AO3

Evolutionary explanation

Preference for sweetness – signals high-energy food.

Preference for salt – needed for many cell functions, appears early.

Preference for fat – high calories, usually unavailable in distant past so valuable.

Neophobia

Innate unwillingness to try unfamiliar foods that could cause harm.

Taste aversion

Innate ability to quickly learn to dislike harmful foods (biological preparedness, Seligman).

Bitterness aversion – adaptive because sign of toxins, benefits survival to avoid.

(+) Research support – prefer high-fat foods during stress, fuels fight-or-flight.

(+) Plausible mechanism – preferences are adaptive response to gut microbes (Alcock *et al.*).

(−) Individual differences – insensitivity to PROP inherited, difficult to explain.

(−) Neophobia now maladaptive – food now generally safe, so just restricts variety.

(−) Cultural influences – major role but ignored by evolutionary explanations.

1 A food preference being 'adaptive' means it:
(a) Is flexible.
(b) Promotes survival.
(c) Is disadvantageous.

2 Preference for fat is adaptive because it:
(a) Contains sugar.
(b) Is high in calories.
(c) Tastes bitter.

3 Neophobia is:
(a) Innate.
(b) Learned.
(c) Neither.

4 An example of a taste aversion is:
(a) Salt.
(b) Sweetness.
(c) Bitterness.

5 Humans have a greater preference for high-fat foods:
(a) During times of stress.
(b) In the summer.
(c) At weekends.

6 A major influence ignored by evolutionary explanations is:
(a) Genes.
(b) Taste aversion.
(c) Culture.

7 Neophobia these days:
(a) Is adaptive.
(b) Ensures a balanced diet.
(c) Restricts dietary variety.

8 It is difficult for evolutionary theories to explain:
(a) Why bitterness aversion is adaptive.
(b) PROP insensitivity.
(c) Why preference for fat is adaptive.

Topic 6: EATING BEHAVIOUR

Answers
1B 2B 3A 4C
5A 6C 7C 8B

Possible extended writing questions:
- Outline and evaluate **one** evolutionary explanation for food preferences. *[AL = 16]*
- Discuss the evolutionary explanation for food preferences. Refer in your answer to neophobia **and** taste aversion. *[AL = 16]*

Explanations for food preferences: Role of learning

Book-link

Y2/A Student Book
Pages 226–227

Y2/A Revision Guide
Pages 138–139

AO1

Classical conditioning – associate new flavour with one we like (flavour-flavour learning).

Operant conditioning – kids' preferences reinforced by parents (e.g. rewards).

Social influences

Family members are role models for eating behaviour (SLT).

Peers and media – also major social influences, especially for older children.

Cultural influences

Cultural norms influence preferences (e.g. meat eating).

Classical conditioning and vicarious reinforcement involved.

AO3

⊖ Classical conditioning – more important in learning aversions than preferences.

⊖ Social influences mostly short-term – effects of TV not as long-lasting as family and peers (Hare-Bruun et al.).

⊕ Multiple influences – chilli-liking shows role of many social/cultural influences.

⊕ Support for SLT – children preferred drink enjoyed by teacher (vicarious) (Jansen and Tenney).

⊕ Research support – cultural changes in fast food, now more food eaten outside home.

Spec Spotlight

Explanations for food preferences: the role of learning in food preference, including social and cultural influences.

Explanations for food preferences. Role of learning – *multiple choice questions*

1 Associating a new flavour with one we like is an example of:
(a) Operant conditioning.
(b) Social learning.
(c) Classical conditioning.

2 Important role models for eating are:
(a) Textbook writers.
(b) Family members.
(c) Police officers.

3 Important social influences on food preferences are:
(a) Brain areas.
(b) Peers and the media.
(c) Genes.

4 A cultural influence on food preferences is:
(a) Norms.
(b) Genes.
(c) Bert's.

5 Multiple social and cultural influences are shown by:
(a) Liking of fats.
(b) Liking for chilli.
(c) Innate dislike of bitterness.

6 The strongest influence of classical conditioning is on:
(a) Food preferences.
(b) Food aversions.
(c) Social learning.

7 Children preferring a drink a teacher enjoyed is the result of:
(a) Classical conditioning.
(b) Evolution.
(c) Vicarious reinforcement.

8 The effects of TV on food preferences are:
(a) Relatively short-term.
(b) Long-lasting.
(c) Non-existent.

Answers
1C 2B 3B 4A
5B 6B 7C 8A

Topic 6: EATING BEHAVIOUR

Possible extended writing questions:

- Outline and evaluate the role of learning in food preference. *[AL = 16]*
- Discuss the roles of social **and** cultural influences in food preferences. *[AL = 16]*

A01

Neural and hormonal mechanisms in eating behaviour

A03

Neural mechanisms

Hypothalamus controls neural/hormonal mechanisms.

Dual-centre model – LH and VMH provide homeostatic control.

Lateral hypothalamus (LH) – on-switch, activates hunger when glucose falls, secretes NPY.

Ventromedial hypothalamus (VMH) – off-switch, triggers satiety as glucose rises.

Spec Spotlight

Neural and hormonal mechanisms involved in the control of eating behaviour, including the role of the hypothalamus, ghrelin and leptin.

Hormonal mechanisms

Ghrelin secreted when stomach empty, stimulates appetite.

Leptin – increases with fat level and satiety, suppresses appetite.

(+) Research support – VMH lesions in rats cause overeating and obesity (Hetherington and Ranson).

(−) Oversimplified – many more biological influences (e.g. CCK), complex picture.

(−) Social and cultural influences – determine normal meal onset.

(−) Based on animal research – eating behaviour more complex in humans than rats.

(+) Real-life application – knowledge to tackle 'obesity crisis', saving lives and money.

Neural and hormonal mechanisms in eating behaviour – *multiple choice questions*

1 Neural and hormonal mechanisms of eating are controlled by the:
(a) Adrenal glands.
(b) Pancreas.
(c) Hypothalamus.

2 The main model of this mechanism is:
(a) Mono-centre model.
(b) Play-centre model.
(c) Dual-centre model.

3 The on-switch of the neural mechanism is the:
(a) Lateral hypothalamus.
(b) Ventromedial hypothalamus.
(c) One on the wall, by the door.

4 A key hormone suppressing appetite is:
(a) Ghrelin.
(b) Leptin.
(c) NPY.

5 Lesions to the VMH in rats can cause:
(a) Anorexia.
(b) Obesity.
(c) Starvation.

6 Normal eating behaviour is controlled mostly by:
(a) Social and cultural factors.
(b) Genes.
(c) The brain.

7 Much research into neural and hormonal mechanisms is:
(a) Animal studies.
(b) Correlational.
(c) Based on self-report methods.

8 Knowledge of neural and hormonal mechanisms can help:
(a) Family influences on anorexia.
(b) Solve the 'obesity crisis'.
(c) Cognitive factors in obesity.

Answers
1C 2C 3A 4B
5B 6A 7A 8B

Possible extended writing questions:

- Describe and evaluate neural **and/or** hormonal mechanisms involved in the control of eating behaviour. *[AL = 16]*
- Discuss the roles of the hypothalamus, ghrelin **and** leptin in the control of eating behaviour. *[AL = 16]*

Biological explanations for anorexia nervosa

Book-link

Y2/A Student Book
Pages 230–231

Y2/A Revision Guide
Pages 142–143

Spec Spotlight

Biological explanations for anorexia nervosa, including genetic and neural explanations.

AO1

Genetic explanation

MZ twins 65% concordance, DZs 32% (Treasure and Holland).

Candidate genes – many have been found linked to AN, e.g. *Ephx2*.

Genome-wide studies – 72 possible genes (Boraska *et al.*), none significantly related to AN.

Neural explanation

Indirect studies using metabolites of serotonin (5-HIAA) and dopamine (HVA).

Serotonin – low levels 5-HIAA, return to normal after short-term weight gain (Attia *et al.*).

Dopamine – low HVA levels in AN patients (e.g. Kaye *et al.*), may reduce anxiety levels.

AO3

⊖ Incorrect assumptions – MZ/DZ twins not treated equally similarly.

⊖ AN is polygenic – single-gene studies futile, many genes make small contributions.

⊕ Research support – dopamine levels lower in recovered patients, suggests cause (Kaye *et al.*).

⊖ Other neurotransmitters – GABA and noradrenaline involved (Nunn *et al.*).

⊖ Not just genes – diathesis-stress wider context, non-biological triggers.

1 The genetics of anorexia have mostly been studied with:
(a) Laboratory experiments.
(b) Twin studies.
(c) Questionnaires.

2 One candidate gene linked to anorexia is:
(a) *Dsc3*.
(b) *Hsp70*.
(c) *Ephx2*.

3 One type of study to identify genes in anorexia is called:
(a) Gnome-wide.
(b) Genome-wide.
(c) Ohm-wide.

4 Anorexia is associated with:
(a) Serotonin underactivity.
(b) Dopamine overactivity.
(c) Serotonin overactivity.

5 Twin studies may wrongly assume that:
(a) DZ twins are treated as similarly as MZs.
(b) MZs are treated more similarly.
(c) DZs are treated more similarly.

6 Anorexia is probably partially caused by:
(a) Many genes making small contributions.
(b) A few significant genes.
(c) A single gene.

7 Dopamine levels in recovered anorexia patients are:
(a) The same as in controls.
(b) Lower than in controls.
(c) Higher than in controls.

8 Other neurotransmitters involved in anorexia include:
(a) Adrenaline.
(b) Testosterone.
(c) GABA.

Answers
1B 2C 3B 4A
5A 6A 7B 8C

Possible extended writing questions:
- Discuss **one or more** biological explanation(s) for anorexia nervosa. *[AL = 16]*
- Outline and evaluate genetic **and/or** neural explanations for anorexia nervosa. *[AL = 16]*

Spec Spotlight

Psychological explanations for anorexia nervosa: family systems theory, including enmeshment, autonomy and control.

Family systems theory (FST) – psychodynamic, Minuchin *et al.* identified four features of complex family system.

(1) **Enmeshment** – family over-involved, assert independence by not eating.

(2) **Overprotective** – family members defend each other from external threats.

(3) **Rigidity** – interactions inflexible, deny need for change, cannot adapt to stress.

(4) **Conflict avoidance** – family actively prevents or suppresses conflict.

Autonomy and **control** (Bruch) – AN caused by daughter's struggle to be independent.

⊕ Research support – AN patients show disturbances of autonomy (Brockmeyer *et al.*).

⊖ Inconsistent evidence – AN families no different from non-AN in enmeshment Aragona *et al.*).

⊕ Successful behavioural therapies – reducing parental control over eating helps recovery.

⊖ Cause and effect – enmeshment, etc. may be result not cause of AN in the family.

⊕ Explains some features – e.g. more common in females and adolescence.

Topic 6: EATING BEHAVIOUR

1 Family systems theory arose from which approach in psychology?
(a) Biological.
(b) Cognitive.
(c) Psychodynamic.

2 'Family too involved with each other' is a description of:
(a) Enmeshment.
(b) Conflict avoidance.
(c) Overprotectiveness.

3 'Inflexible interactions' is a feature of:
(a) Rigidity.
(b) Enmeshment.
(c) Autonomy.

4 Which is *not* a feature of Minuchin *et al.*'s family systems theory:
(a) Overprotective.
(b) Rigidity.
(c) Autonomy.

5 Research shows AN patients:
(a) Have high self-esteem.
(b) Are highly independent.
(c) Have disturbances of autonomy.

6 The evidence related to the theory is best described as:
(a) Highly supportive.
(b) Inconsistent.
(c) Rubbish.

7 One benefit of family systems theory is:
(a) Better knowledge of biological influences.
(b) Consistent therapy.
(c) Useful therapy.

8 Family systems theory explains:
(a) The genetic basis of anorexia.
(b) Why anorexia is more common in females.
(c) The neural basis of anorexia.

Answers
1C 2A 3A 4C
5C 6B 7C 8B

Topic 6: EATING BEHAVIOUR

Possible extended writing questions:

- Outline and evaluate the family systems theory of anorexia nervosa. Refer to enmeshment in your answer. *[AL = 16]*
- Discuss **one** biological and **one** psychological explanation for anorexia nervosa. *[AL = 16]*

Book-link

Y2/A Student Book
Pages 234–235

Y2/A Revision Guide
Pages 146–147

Spec Spotlight

Psychological
explanations for
anorexia nervosa:
social learning theory,
including modelling,
reinforcement and
media.

Psychological explanations for anorexia nervosa: SLT

A01

Social learning theory (SLT)
Direct – classical and operant conditioning.
Indirect – observation and modelling.

Modelling – observing and imitating real
person (e.g. family) or in the media (e.g. TV).

Vicarious **reinforcement** – observe model
rewarded, increases chance of imitation.

Media – transmits cultural ideals of body
shape, vicariously reinforced (e.g. fame).

Key study: Dittmar et al.

Procedure – girls shown images of Barbie/
Emme dolls.

Findings – girls more dissatisfied with own
body-shape after seeing Barbie images, lower
body-esteem.

A03

⊕ Research support – AN in girls on Fiji
related to media access (Becker et al.).

⊕ Cultural changes – AN increasing in
Japan related to Western media (Chisuwa
and O'Dea).

⊖ Can't explain why not more common –
most young women exposed to thin
models but no AN (diathesis?).

⊕ Explains gender differences – 'bigorexia'
in men due to media.

⊖ Real-life application – provides models of
healthy eating behaviour.

Psychological explanations for anorexia nervosa. SLT – *multiple choice questions*

Topic 6: EATING BEHAVIOUR

1 Social learning involves:
   (a) Classical conditioning only.
   (b) Modelling only.
   (c) Direct and indirect learning.

2 Imitating a model because they have been rewarded is:
   (a) Classical conditioning.
   (b) Operant conditioning.
   (c) Vicarious reinforcement.

3 A key source of vicarious reinforcement in AN is:
   (a) Politicians.
   (b) The media.
   (c) Teachers.

4 Dittmar *et al.* showed girls images of:
   (a) People with anorexia.
   (b) Barbie and Emme dolls.
   (c) People with obesity.

5 Support for SLT comes from a study of girls in:
   (a) Finland.
   (b) France.
   (c) Fiji.

6 SLT can explain:
   (a) Very little about AN.
   (b) Increased AN in Japan.
   (c) Why most young women do not develop AN.

7 There is an eating disorder in men called:
   (a) Bigorexia.
   (b) Largeorexia.
   (c) Hugeorexia.

8 Successful SLT-based treatment has used:
   (a) Models of healthy eating.
   (b) Drugs.
   (c) Surgery.

Answers
1C 2C 3B 4B
5C 6B 7A 8A

Possible extended writing questions:

- Discuss the social learning theory explanation for anorexia nervosa. Refer in your answer to modelling, reinforcement **and** media. *[AL = 16]*
- Outline and evaluate **two** psychological explanations for anorexia nervosa. *[AL = 16]*

Book-link

Y2/A Student Book
Pages 236–237

Y2/A Revision Guide
Pages 148–149

Psychological explanations for anorexia nervosa: Cognitive theory

AO1

Distortions – of body image, may cause AN, three influential factors.

(1) Disturbed perceptions of body shape and weight – lead to food restriction.

Overestimate body weight/size – less accurate than controls (Williamson *et al.*).

(2) **Irrational beliefs** – defy logic, create automatic negative thoughts (Beck).

Perfectionism – key irrational belief, must meet demanding standards in life.

(3) Cognitive inflexibility – e.g. difficulty in set-shifting tasks, apply same skills where no longer useful.

AO3

⊕ Support for distortions – brain scans show less activation when viewing own body (Sachdev *et al.*).

⊕ Further support – perfectionism is childhood predictor of later AN (Halmi *et al.*).

⊖ Contradictory research – body size estimates no different AN/no AN (Cornelissen *et al.*).

⊕ Real-life application – enhanced CBT can lead to long-term recovery (Grave *et al.*).

⊖ Cause and effect – inflexibility a result of AN not a cause (Shott *et al.*).

Spec Spotlight

Psychological explanations for anorexia nervosa: cognitive theory, including distortions and irrational beliefs.

Psychological explanations for anorexia nervosa. Cognitive theory – *multiple choice questions*

1 A major psychological cause of AN is:
(a) Genetics.
(b) Cognitive distortions.
(c) Neurochemistry.

2 A common tendency of people with AN is to:
(a) Overestimate their body size.
(b) Binge eat.
(c) Have high self-esteem.

3 Perfectionism is an example of:
(a) A disturbed perception.
(b) An irrational belief.
(c) A biological explanation.

4 Failing to adapt to changing situations is the result of:
(a) Rational belief.
(b) Anorexia.
(c) Cognitive inflexibility.

5 People with AN may have distorted perceptions of:
(a) Everything.
(b) Their own body size.
(c) Body sizes in general.

6 Cognitive research shows that a key predictor of adult AN is:
(a) Perfectionism in childhood.
(b) Having a twin with AN.
(c) Serotonin levels.

7 One application of cognitive theory is:
(a) Cognitive behaviour therapy.
(b) Drug treatments.
(c) Brain surgery.

8 According to Shott *et al.*, cognitive inflexibility:
(a) Causes anorexia.
(b) Is not linked to anorexia.
(c) Is caused by anorexia.

Answers
1B 2A 3B 4C
5B 6A 7A 8C

Topic 6: EATING BEHAVIOUR

Possible extended writing questions:

- Describe and evaluate the cognitive theory of anorexia nervosa. Refer in your answer to distortions **and** irrational beliefs. *[AL = 16]*
- Discuss **two or more** psychological explanations of anorexia nervosa. *[AL = 16]*

Spec Spotlight

Biological
explanations for obesity,
including genetic and
neural explanations.

Genetic explanation

Obesity (measured by body mass index) runs
in families.

Family patterns – family studies (20–50%
concordance) and twin studies (61–80%).

Polygenetic – many interacting genes with
small effects, e.g. 97 genes (Locke *et al.*).

⊖ Inconclusive studies – MZ and DZ twins
not treated equally similarly.

⊖ Contradictory evidence – leptin-related
genes not involved (Paracchini *et al.*).

Neural explanation

Serotonin regulates eating, dopamine involved
in reward.

Serotonin – low levels from inherited
dysfunction, inaccurate satiety signals.

Dopamine – low levels so can't perform usual
reward function from eating.

⊕ Support for serotonin – mice with no 2C
receptors develop obesity (Ohia *et al.*).

⊕ Support for dopamine – DRD2 gene
involved, less dopamine-linked reward.

⊕ Real-life application – future treatments
such as drugs targeting serotonin/
dopamine.

1 Twin and family studies measure inheritance of obesity with:
(a) Concordance rates.
(b) Conventional rates.
(c) Con carne rates.

2 The most likely genetic explanation of obesity is:
(a) It is caused by one gene.
(b) Many genes have small effects.
(c) Some genes have big effects.

3 Low levels of serotonin result in:
(a) Inaccurate satiety signals.
(b) Weight loss.
(c) Inhibition of eating.

4 Dopamine levels in obesity are:
(a) Higher than normal.
(b) The same as normal.
(c) Lower than normal.

5 Paracchini *et al.* found that leptin-related genes:
(a) Cause obesity.
(b) Are not involved in obesity.
(c) Do not exist.

6 What did Ohia *et al.* link to obesity?
(a) Concordance rates.
(b) Serotonin 2C receptors.
(c) Dopamine receptors.

7 The specific gene linked to obesity is:
(a) R2D2.
(b) DRD1.
(c) DRD2.

8 Possible obesity treatments based on neural explanations include:
(a) Drugs.
(b) Cognitive behaviour therapy.
(c) Counselling.

Answers
1A 2B 3A 4C
5B 6B 7C 8A

Possible extended writing questions:
- Discuss **one** biological explanation for obesity. *[AL = 16]*
- Outline and evaluate genetic **and/or** neural explanations for obesity. *[AL = 16]*

A01

Psychological explanations for obesity

A03

Restraint theory

Herman and Polivy – restricting food intake is self-defeating, think about food a lot.

Paradoxical outcome – preoccupied with food, disinhibited eating, weight gain.

Disinhibition

Restrained eating makes you sensitive to food-related cues.

Leads to disinhibited eating, maintained by distorted thinking (e.g. all-or-none).

Boundary model

Herman and Polivy – aversive states, hunger motivates eating, satiety (discomfort) motivates to stop.

Zone of biological indifference – neither hungry nor full, wider in restrained eaters, more of eating under cognitive control.

(+) Research support – restrained eaters ate more (Wardle and Beales).

(+) Role of media – restrained eaters ate more after seeing images of thinness (Boyce and Kuijer).

(−) Contradictory evidence – restrained eating did lead to weight loss (Savage *et al.*).

(−) Restraint multifaceted – only rigid restraint type (not flexible type) linked to obesity (Savage *et al.*).

(+) Real-life application – restraint leads to disinhibition (boundary model), better than 'quick fix' diets.

Spec Spotlight

Psychological explanations for obesity, including restraint theory, disinhibition and the boundary model.

1 Restrained eating is self-defeating because:
(a) You lose weight.
(b) You eat fewer calories.
(c) You think about food a lot.

2 Sensitivity to food-related cues leads to:
(a) Allergies.
(b) Disinhibited eating.
(c) Weight loss.

3 Hunger and satiety are:
(a) Under biological control in restrained eaters.
(b) Biologically aversive states.
(c) Accurately perceived in dieters.

4 In the zone of biological indifference:
(a) Cognitive factors dominate.
(b) Dieters eat when hungry.
(c) Dieters stop eating when full.

5 Wardle and Beales found that:
(a) Media images influenced eating.
(b) Restraint theory lacks validity.
(c) Restrained eaters ate more.

6 Savage *et al.* found that restrained eating led to:
(a) Weight loss.
(b) Weight gain.
(c) Variable outcomes.

7 The type of restraint *not* linked to obesity is:
(a) Flexible.
(b) Rigid.
(c) Paradoxical.

8 The boundary model:
(a) Has no real-life application.
(b) Encourages food restriction.
(c) Is a useful alternative to 'quick fix' diets.

Answers
1C 2B 3B 4A
5C 6A 7A 8C

Possible extended writing questions:
- Outline and evaluate **two or more** psychological explanations for obesity. *[AL = 16]*
- Discuss restraint theory **and one other** psychological explanation for obesity. *[AL = 16]*

Explanations for the success and failure of dieting

Book-link

Y2/A Student Book
Pages 242–243

Y2/A Revision Guide
Pages 154–155

Spec Spotlight

Explanations for the success and failure of dieting.

AO1

Spiral model (Heatherton and Polivy) – diet failure creates sense of personal deficiency, low self-esteem.

Downward spiral – try harder, more distress, oversensitive to food cues , more eating.

Ironic processes (Wegner *et al.*) – diet increases food preoccupation (white bear), paradoxical.

Distraction doesn't work – use all your attention not to think about food, self-defeating (and ironic).

Restraint – leads to eating under cognitive control, and disinhibition.

Boundary model – don't eat when hungry or when feeling full, have a preset limit and then carry on eating ('might as well').

AO3

⊕ Practical uses – spiral model suggests addressing low self-esteem issues.

⊕ Research support – strong ironic rebound effect (Adriaanse *et al.*).

⊖ Minimal effects – ironic processes exaggerated in lab experiments.

⊕ Real-life application – ironic processes theory suggests paying full attention to eating (Boon *et al.*).

⊖ Individual differences – some lose weight even when preoccupied with food (Ogden).

1 The cycle of diet failure and low self-esteem is explained by the:
(a) Spiral model.
(b) Ironic processes theory.
(c) Boundary model.

2 According to ironic processes theory, the outcome of dieting is:
(a) Weight loss.
(b) Success.
(c) Paradoxical.

3 Restrained eating is:
(a) Under biological control.
(b) An excellent way to lose weight.
(c) Under cognitive control.

4 Dieters:
(a) Eat when they feel hungry.
(b) Stop eating when they feel full.
(c) Set themselves an artificial intake limit.

5 Self-esteem issues should be addressed, according to the:
(a) Ironic processes theory.
(b) Spiral model.
(c) Boundary model.

6 The effects of ironic processes are:
(a) Greater in the lab than in real-life.
(b) Very significant in real-life.
(c) Non-existent.

7 According to ironic processes theory, dieters should:
(a) Give eating their full attention.
(b) Improve their self-esteem.
(c) Eat little and often.

8 All three theories have trouble explaining:
(a) Why dieting fails.
(b) Individual differences.
(c) How to achieve weight loss.

Answers
1A 2C 3C 4C
5B 6A 7A 8B

Possible extended writing questions:

- Discuss explanations for the success and failure of dieting. *[AL = 16]*
- Describe and evaluate **one or more** explanations for the success and failure of dieting. *[AL = 16]*

Y2/A Student Book
Pages 254–255
Y2/A Revision Guide
Pages 156–157

General adaptation syndrome (GAS)

(1) Alarm reaction – sympathetic ANS, adrenaline/noradrenaline, fight or flight.

(2) Resistance – adapt to combat stressor, resources used up, parasympathetic.

(3) Exhaustion – adaptation fails, resources drained, stress-related illnesses.

⊕ Support for GAS – rats showed same response to various stressors (Selye).

⊖ Not general response – monkeys' responses depend on stressor (Mason).

Spec Spotlight

The physiology of stress, including general adaptation syndrome, the hypothalamic pituitary-adrenal system, the sympathomedullary pathway and the role of cortisol.

Physiological stress response

Sympathomedullary pathway (acute) – fight/flight, involves adrenaline and adrenal medulla.

Hypothalamic pituitary-adrenal system (chronic) – involves ACTH and adrenal cortex.

Cortisol – stress hormone, affects glucose metabolism, restores energy, feedback.

⊖ Androcentric bias – female response is tend and befriend, not fight or flight (Taylor).

⊖ Ignores psychological factors – response depends on cognitive appraisals (Lazarus).

⊕ Real-life benefits – Addison's treated with cortisol, increased during stress.

1 GAS stands for:
(a) General adaptive system.
(b) General alternative syndrome.
(c) General adaptation syndrome.

2 Triggering fight or flight is a feature of the:
(a) Alarm reaction.
(b) Resistance.
(c) Exhaustion.

3 The chronic stress response is controlled by the:
(a) Hypothalamic-pituitary-adrenal system.
(b) Sympathomedullary pathway.
(c) Fight or flight response.

4 The main acute stress hormone is:
(a) Cortisol.
(b) Glucose.
(c) ACTH.

5 Selye used which animals in his research?
(a) Cats.
(b) Rats.
(c) Humans.

6 Mason argued that the stress response:
(a) Is a general response.
(b) Differs in men and women.
(c) Varies depending on the stressor.

7 The stress response of females is:
(a) Fight or flight.
(b) Tend and befriend.
(c) Identical to that of males.

8 Knowledge of stress physiology has been used to help treat:
(a) Addison's disease.
(b) Atkinson's disease.
(c) Aitchison's disease.

Possible extended writing questions:

- Discuss the physiology of stress. *[AL = 16]*
- Describe and evaluate the general adaptation syndrome. *[AL = 16]*
- Outline and evaluate the role of the hypothalamic-pituitary-adrenal system, the sympathomedullary pathway **and** cortisol in the response to stress. *[AL = 16]*

Y2/A Student Book
Pages 256–257
Y2/A Revision Guide
Pages 158–159

Spec Spotlight

The role of stress in illness, including reference to immunosuppression and cardiovascular disorders.

Immunosuppression

Cortisol (direct) and lifestyle (indirect) suppress immune system.

Chronic stress (exams) – decrease in NK and killer T cells (Kiecolt-Glaser et al.).

Caring for relative – increased immune antibodies, illness and depression.

Cardiovascular disorders

Stress has acute and chronic effects on CVDs.

Acute – watching football match, more heart attacks from emotional arousal (Wilbert-Lampen et al.).

Chronic – workplace stress linked to heart attack (INTERHEART study).

⊖ Increased immunity – mild stressors enhanced immune response in rats (Dharbhar).

⊕ Research support – link between immunosuppression and cancer (Pereira et al.).

⊖ Indirect link – stress increases heart attack risk but may not cause it.

⊕ Real-life benefits – low doses of stress hormones before surgery help recovery.

⊖ Artificial stressors – short-term controlled studies lack external validity.

1 Which of these has a direct effect on the immune system?
(a) Cortisol.
(b) Smoking.
(c) Poor diet.

2 Chronic exam stress leads to:
(a) Increased killer T cells.
(b) No change in NK cells.
(c) Decreased NK cells.

3 Sudden emotional arousal is an example of:
(a) Chronic stress.
(b) Acute stress.
(c) Long-term stress.

4 Which is a study of workplace stress?
(a) Kiecolt-Glaser *et al.*
(b) Wilbert-Lampen *et al.*
(c) INTERHEART.

5 Some research with rats has shown that stressors:
(a) Have no effect on immunity.
(b) Are immunoenhancing.
(c) Cause cancer.

6 The relationship between stress and CVDs/heart attacks is:
(a) Indirect.
(b) Direct.
(c) Non-existent.

7 Recovery after surgery can be helped using:
(a) Sudden shocks.
(b) High doses of cortisol.
(c) Low dose of stress hormones.

8 Controlled studies of short-term stressors:
(a) Lack external validity.
(b) Lack internal validity.
(c) Have high internal validity.

Answers
1A 2C 3B 4C
5B 6A 7C 8A

Possible extended writing questions:

- Outline and evaluate the role of stress in illness. *[AL = 16]*
- Discuss the role of stress in illness. Refer in your answer to immunosuppression **and/or** cardiovascular disorders. *[AL = 16]*

Book-link

Y2/A Student Book
Pages 258–259

Y2/A Revision Guide
Pages 160–161

Spec Spotlight

Sources of stress:
life changes.

AO1

Major infrequent positive or negative events
(marriage, death) (Holmes and Rahe).

Adjustment required – makes it stressful
because have to adapt to change.

SRRS – measured with Social Readjustment
Rating Scale, Life Change Units (LCUs).

More than 300 LCUs means 80% likelihood of
illness in following year.

Key study: Rahe et al.

Procedure – US sailors, life changes six months
before duty, illness record on board.

Findings – significant positive correlation
(+.118) between LCUs and illness scores.

AO3

⊕ Research support – prospective studies
predict illness from life changes
(Lietzén et al.).

⊖ Ignores individual differences – impact of
life changes depends on perception.

⊖ Nature of change – positive changes on
SRRS less stressful than negative.

⊖ Life changes unimportant – daily hassles
better predictors of illness (Lazarus).

⊖ Correlational research – can't conclude
stress of life changes causes illness.

1 Life changes are:
(a) Minor but common events.
(b) Always negative events.
(c) Big but infrequent events.

2 Life changes are measured with:
(a) Social readjustment rating scale.
(b) Stress readjustment rating scale.
(c) Social reality rating scale.

3 LCU stands for:
(a) Like change unit.
(b) Lite change unit.
(c) Life change unit.

4 The correlation found by Rahe *et al.* was:
(a) −.118
(b) +.118
(c) Not significant.

5 Strong support for life changes comes from:
(a) Retrospective studies.
(b) Prospective research.
(c) Lab experiments.

6 Negative changes on the SRRS are:
(a) Less stressful than positive ones.
(b) Just as stressful as positive ones.
(c) More stressful than positive ones.

7 Life changes are _____ as daily hassles.
(a) Just as important.
(b) Less important.
(c) More important.

8 Most research into the stress of life changes is:
(a) Correlational.
(b) Experimental.
(c) Observational.

Answers
1C 2A 3C 4B
5B 6C 7B 8A

Possible extended writing questions:
- Discuss research into **one or more** sources of stress. *[AL = 16]*
- Outline and evaluate life changes as a source of stress. *[AL = 16]*

Sources of stress: Daily hassles

Spec Spotlight

Sources of stress:
daily hassles.

AO1

Frequent everyday irritations, effects add up so stressful (Lazarus *et al.*).

Stress of hassles depends on our psychological appraisal (primary and secondary).

HSUP – measured with Hassles and Uplifts Scale, uplifts are everyday positives/pleasures.

Daily hassles are proximal – immediate and direct effects (unlike life changes).

Key study: Kanner *et al.*

Procedure – 100 participants, completed several scales in 9 months.

Findings – significant positive correlation, the more hassles, the more severe the psychological symptoms.

AO3

⊕ Research support – hassles better predictors of illness than life changes.

⊖ Retrospective research – validity depends on accuracy of memories.

⊖ Less effect than life changes – hassles only stressful during life changes (amplification).

⊖ Can't explain gender differences – males and females differ in perception of hassles.

⊖ Correlational research – can't claim that stress of hassles causes illness (indirect).

1 Daily hassles are:
(a) Very significant events.
(b) Rare and unusual.
(c) Relatively minor but frequent.

2 The two forms of psychological appraisal are:
(a) Primary and secondary.
(b) Secondary and tertiary.
(c) Tertiary and quaternary.

3 'Hassles are proximal' means they:
(a) Are indirect sources of stress.
(b) Have direct immediate effects.
(c) Are like life changes.

4 Hassles and psychological symptoms were studied by:
(a) Kiecolt-Glaser et al.
(b) Rahe et al.
(c) Kanner et al.

5 Hassles are _____ predictors of illness than life changes.
(a) Better.
(b) Worse.
(c) Much worse.

6 Research that relies on people's memories of hassles is:
(a) Prospective.
(b) Observational.
(c) Retrospective.

7 Hassles affect health only during life changes, according to the:
(a) Abbreviation hypothesis.
(b) Amplification hypothesis.
(c) Amputation hypothesis.

8 Hassles theory struggles to explain:
(a) Correlation between stress and illness.
(b) Gender differences.
(c) Gender similarities.

Answers
1C 2A 3B 4C
5A 6C 7B 8B

Possible extended writing questions:
- Outline and evaluate research into daily hassles as a source of stress. [AL = 16]
- Discuss daily hassles **and one other** source of stress. [AL = 16]

Spec Spotlight

Sources of stress:
workplace stress,
including the effects
of workload and
control.

AO1

Workload and control affect amount of stress experienced.

Job demands-control model – demands cause stress but depends on control.

Control: Bosma et al.

Procedure – workload and control assessed in UK civil servants.

Findings – job demands are not a stressor, but low control is linked with CHD over 5 years.

Workload and control: Johansson et al.

Procedure – natural experiment, sawmill workers (finishers and cleaners).

Findings – more stress hormones, illness, absenteeism in finishers (no control).

AO3

⊕ Simplistic model – complex interactions of many more than just two factors.

⊕ Cultural differences – lack of control not so stressful in collectivist cultures (Györkös et al.).

⊖ Job control may be stressful – people with low self-efficacy stressed by control (Meier et al.).

⊕ Methodological issues – lower-grade civil servants less job security (confounding variable).

⊖ Methodological issues – sawmill study no random allocation, groups differed.

Topic 7: STRESS

1 The main workplace stressors are:
(a) Life changes.
(b) Workload and control.
(c) Daily hassles.

2 Bosma *et al.* studied:
(a) Students.
(b) Civil servants.
(c) Sawmill workers.

3 Bosma *et al.* found that:
(a) High control was more stressful.
(b) Job demands caused stress.
(c) Low control was linked with illness.

4 Johansson *et al.*'s study was a:
(a) Field experiment.
(b) Observational study.
(c) Natural experiment.

5 A problem with the job demands-control model is that it is:
(a) Outdated.
(b) Simplistic.
(c) Too complex.

6 Lack of control is *not* stressful in:
(a) Collectivist cultures.
(b) Urban cultures.
(c) Individualist cultures.

7 People with low self-efficacy:
(a) Find lack of control stressful.
(b) Find having control stressful.
(c) Are not interested in control.

8 A problem in the sawmill study was:
(a) No job security.
(b) Cultural differences.
(c) No random allocation to experimental groups.

Answers
1B 2B 3C 4C
5B 6A 7B 8C

Possible extended writing questions:
- Discuss research into workplace stress. *[AL = 16]*
- Describe and evaluate workload **and/or** control as sources of workplace stress. *[AL = 16]*

Topic 7: STRESS

Self-report measures

Social Readjustment Rating Scale (SRRS) – measures 43 positive and negative life events.

⊖ Ambiguous items – some items vague and open to differing interpretations.

Stress measured by LCUs – values for all events of last 12 months added for score.

⊖ Contamination effect – items overlap with symptoms, reflect illness not predict it.

Hassles Scale – 117 items from various categories, severity on 3-point scale.

⊖ Assess 'global' stress – single score does not reflect types of hassle/change.

Uplifts Scale – 135 items, uplifts offset stressful effects of hassles.

⊖ Muddles events – only uncontrollable changes predict illness (Stern *et al.*).

Physiological measures

Sweat caused by ANS arousal conducts electricity.

⊖ Individual differences – labiles produce many more resting SCRs than stabiles.

Skin conductance response (SCR) – tonic measures baseline, phasic measures electrical conduction.

Spec Spotlight

Measuring stress: self-report scales (Social Readjustment Rating Scale and Hassles and Uplifts Scale) and physiological measures, including skin conductance response.

1 The SRRS measures how many life events?
(a) 23
(b) 33
(c) 43

2 In the SRRS, LCUs are added up for the previous:
(a) 6 months.
(b) 12 months.
(c) 18 months.

3 The Hassles Scale measures severity on a:
(a) True/false scale.
(b) 7-point scale.
(c) 3-point scale.

4 Skin conductance response is a:
(a) Physiological measure of stress.
(b) Self-report measure of stress.
(c) Psychological measure of stress.

5 Validity of self-report scales is reduced by the:
(a) Condemnation effect.
(b) Contamination effect.
(c) Consternation effect.

6 Self-report scales assess 'global' stress because they:
(a) Provide a single score.
(b) Are used all over the world.
(c) Are printed on round paper.

7 According to Stern et al., illness is predicted on the SRRS by:
(a) Uncontrollable events.
(b) Every item.
(c) Predictable events.

8 Labiles produce _____ resting SCRs than stabiles.
(a) More.
(b) Fewer.
(c) The same number of.

Answers
1C 2B 3C 4A
5B 6A 7A 8A

Possible extended writing questions:

- Outline and evaluate **two** ways of measuring stress. *[AL = 16]*
- In relation to measuring stress, discuss **one** self-report scale and **one** physiological measure. *[AL = 16]*

Book-link

Y2/A Student Book
Pages 266–267

Y2/A Revision Guide
Pages 168–169

Spec Spotlight

Individual
differences in stress:
personality types A, B
and C and associated
behaviours.

A01

Individual differences in stress: Personality type

A03

Type A – hostile, competitive, time-urgent (Friedman and Rosenman).

Type B – laid back, relaxed, tolerant, less competitive than Type A.

Western Collaborative Group Study – 3000 US males free of CHD at start.

Link to CHD – after 8.5 years 257 men had CHD, 70% were Type A at start, Type A raises physiological stress response.

Type C – pathologically nice people who repress emotions to avoid conflict.

Link with cancer in Vietnam veterans who repressed emotions (Dattore et al.).

⊕ Research support – stroke sufferers more likely Type A (Edigo et al.).

⊖ Contradictory evidence – Type B greater CHD risk than Type A (Ragland and Brand).

⊖ Type A too broad – hostility component linked to CHD (Dembroski et al.).

⊖ Complex link with CHD – classification modified but then the boundary between A and B blurred.

⊖ Contradictory evidence – Type C/cancer link very inconsistent in research.

1 Type ___ people are hostile and competitive.
- (a) A
- (b) B
- (c) C

2 The Western Collaborative Group Study studied:
- (a) 3000 US students.
- (b) 3000 US females.
- (c) 3000 US males.

3 The study found a link between CHD and:
- (a) Type A.
- (b) Type B.
- (c) Type C.

4 Dattore *et al.* studied Type C in:
- (a) Women with cervical cancer.
- (b) Veterans of the Vietnam War.
- (c) Women with breast cancer.

5 Who found stroke sufferers were more likely to be Type A?
- (a) Ragland and Brand.
- (b) Edigo *et al.*
- (c) Demroski *et al.*

6 The Type A component most closely linked to illness is:
- (a) Competitiveness.
- (b) Hostility.
- (c) Time urgency.

7 The link between Type A/B personality and illness is:
- (a) Complex.
- (b) Well-established.
- (c) Non-existent.

8 Research into the Type C/cancer link can be described as:
- (a) Extremely reliable.
- (b) Highly valid.
- (c) Inconsistent.

Answers
1A 2C 3A 4B
5B 6B 7A 8C

Possible extended writing questions:
- Discuss individual differences in stress. *[AL = 16]*
- Outline and evaluate personality types A, B **and** C in relation to individual differences in stress. *[AL = 16]*

Individual differences in stress: Hardiness

individual differences in stress: Hardiness – *multiple choice questions*

1 Hardiness:
(a) Makes stress worse.
(b) Protects against stress.
(c) Makes no difference to the effects of stress.

2 The three dimensions of hardiness are:
(a) Commitment, change, courage.
(b) Commitment, challenge, control.
(c) Commitment, challenge, courage.

3 Kobasa found that hardy managers:
(a) Were less ill.
(b) Could not tolerate stress.
(c) Did not differ from other managers.

4 Maddi studied:
(a) 400 US students.
(b) 400 US teachers.
(c) 400 US managers.

5 According to Funk, hardiness scales may actually measure:
(a) Levels of hardiness.
(b) Levels of Type A.
(c) Lack of neuroticism.

6 Which of the three Cs is most important, according to Hull *et al.*?
(a) Control.
(b) Commitment.
(c) Challenge.

7 Contrada found that hardy students:
(a) Had relatively low blood pressure.
(b) Lacked control over events.
(c) Disliked challenges.

8 It is possible to increase hardiness with:
(a) Varnish.
(b) Drugs.
(c) Training programmes.

Answers
1B 2B 3A 4C
5C 6A 7A 8C

Possible extended writing questions:
- Discuss **two** individual differences in stress. *[AL = 16]*
- Describe and evaluate research into hardiness. In your answer refer to commitment, challenge **and** control. *[AL = 16]*

Book-link

Y2/A Student Book
Pages 270–271

Y2/A Revision Guide
Pages 172–173

Spec Spotlight

Managing and
coping with stress:
drug therapy
(benzodiazepines,
beta blockers).

Managing and coping with stress: Drug therapy

AO1

AO3

Benzodiazepines (BZs)

Reduce anxiety by lowering arousal of CNS.

Mode of action – act on GABA, neuro-transmitter inhibiting CNS activity.

BZ molecules combine with GABA receptors – enhance natural inhibition of brain activity.

(+) Research evidence – review concluded BZs better than placebo (Baldwin *et al.*).

(−) Dependence – BZs should be short-term only, but sometimes taken for years.

(−) Symptoms only treated – good for short-term relief but not for chronic anxiety.

Beta blockers (BBs)

Reduce arousal in sympathetic nervous system.

Mode of action – act on stress hormones adrenaline and noradrenaline.

Prevent beta-adrenergic receptors being stimulated by adrenaline/noradrenaline, slow heart rate, reduce blood pressure.

(+) Research evidence – BBs effective in treating everyday anxieties (Kelly).

(−) Side effects – BBs cause drowsiness and breathing problems, outweighs benefits, therapy may be better.

1 BZs:
(a) Increase sympathetic arousal.
(b) Reduce arousal of the CNS.
(c) Increase activity in the brain.

2 BZs:
(a) Block GABA activity.
(b) Have no effect on GABA.
(c) Enhance GABA activity.

3 BBs act on:
(a) Adrenaline and noradrenaline.
(b) Cortisol and adrenaline.
(c) GABA and noradrenaline.

4 BBs:
(a) Reduce adrenaline levels.
(b) Stimulate beta-adrenergic receptors.
(c) Prevent stimulation of beta-adrenergic receptors.

5 Researcher(s) who found BZs more effective than placebo:
(a) Ashton.
(b) Baldwin et al.
(c) Kelly.

6 BZs taken for months or years can cause:
(a) Less stress to be experienced.
(b) Dependence.
(c) Anxiety to be cured.

7 Side effects of a drug should be weighed up against:
(a) Its benefits.
(b) Other treatments.
(c) Both of the above.

8 BBs and BZs are good for treating:
(a) Acute anxiety.
(b) Chronic anxiety.
(c) Causes of anxiety.

Answers
1B 2C 3A 4C
5B 6B 7C 8A

Possible extended writing questions:

• Discuss **one or more** ways of managing and coping with stress. *[AL = 16]*
• Outline and evaluate drug therapy as a way of managing and coping with stress. *[AL = 16]*

Managing and coping with stress: SIT

Book-link

Y2/A Student Book
Pages 272–273

Y2/A Revision Guide
Pages 174–175

Spec Spotlight

Managing and coping with stress: stress inoculation therapy.

AO1

Stress inoculation therapy (SIT) – a form of cognitive behaviour therapy concerned with how you think about stress (Meichenbaum).

Focus on cognitive appraisal – learn to think of stressors as challenges.

(1) Conceptualisation – client and therapist work to understand stressors.

(2) Skills acquisition and rehearsal – learn skills to cope (e.g. self-statements) and plan ahead.

(3) Real-life application/follow-through – client practices in safe environment, plus feedback.

Relapse prevention – client sees setbacks as learning opportunities, plans strategy.

AO3

⊕ Flexible therapy – variety of stress management methods tailored to need.

⊖ Demanding therapy – big commitment needs motivation, many drop out.

⊖ Depends on control – not all elements equally effective, control is main factor.

⊕ Research support – SIT effective for all levels of stress, improves performance (Saunders *et al.*).

⊕ Emphasises prevention – focuses on root causes and planning, not 'quick fix'.

1 SIT focuses on:
  (a) Central nervous system activity.
  (b) Cognitive appraisal.
  (c) Stress hormones.

2 The second stage of SIT is:
  (a) Skills acquisition and rehearsal.
  (b) Conceptualisation.
  (c) Real-life application.

3 Identifying the client's stressors is part of:
  (a) Conceptualisation.
  (b) Skills acquisition and rehearsal.
  (c) Follow-through.

4 SIT ultimately aims to:
  (a) Stop stress from happening.
  (b) Prevent relapse.
  (c) Lower blood pressure.

5 A major strength of SIT is that it is:
  (a) Quick and easy.
  (b) The same for everyone.
  (c) Flexible.

6 Many people drop out of SIT because:
  (a) It is too inflexible.
  (b) It is a demanding therapy.
  (c) They no longer experience stress.

7 The central effective element of SIT is:
  (a) Control.
  (b) Practice.
  (c) Feedback.

8 SIT is especially useful for:
  (a) Extreme stress.
  (b) Moderate stress.
  (c) All levels of stress.

Answers
1B 2A 3A 4B
5C 6B 7A 8C

Possible extended writing questions:

- Discuss stress inoculation therapy as a way of managing **and** coping with stress. *[AL = 16]*
- Describe and evaluate stress inoculation therapy **and one other** way of managing and coping with stress. *[AL = 16]*

AO1

AO3

Topic 7: STRESS

Book-link

Y2/A Student Book
Pages 274–275

Y2/A Revision Guide
Pages 176–177

Spec Spotlight

Managing and
coping with stress:
biofeedback.

Control involuntary physiological responses,
Budzynski identified three phases.

(1) Awareness of responses – machine
converts activity into signal (e.g. screen).

(2) Learn to control response – use stress
management techniques to change signal.

(3) Transfer to everyday life – no need for
machine, used in stressful situations.

Key study: Davis

Procedure – thirteen 45-minute feedback
sessions over 8 weeks.

Findings – cortisol and anxiety levels lower
after 8-month follow-up.

⊕ Research support – biofeedback reduced
perceived stress over 28 days (Lemaire
et al.).

⊖ Measurement issues – depends what is
measured, little effect on physiological
indicators of stress.

⊕ Improves other methods – relaxation
even more effective with biofeedback.

⊕ Convenience – small wearable devices,
easy to use in real stress situations.

⊖ Individual differences – not suitable for
all, needs motivation and understanding.

Managing and coping with stress: Biofeedback – multiple choice questions

1 Biofeedback aims to control:
(a) The mind.
(b) The planet.
(c) Involuntary responses.

2 In the 2nd phase, the client:
(a) Learns to control the response.
(b) Becomes aware of responses.
(c) Transfers to everyday life.

3 There were _____ sessions in Davis's study.
(a) 45
(b) 8
(c) 13

4 Davis measured:
(a) Perceived stress.
(b) Cortisol and anxiety levels.
(c) Adrenaline and noradrenaline.

5 One study found biofeedback reduced stress over:
(a) 28 hours.
(b) 28 days.
(c) 28 months.

6 Biofeedback has little effect on:
(a) Thursdays.
(b) How stressed people feel.
(c) Physiological indicators of stress.

7 A benefit of biofeedback is that it:
(a) Is a quick treatment.
(b) Is convenient.
(c) Requires no effort.

8 Biofeedback:
(a) Is more effective for some people than for others.
(b) Is suitable for everyone.
(c) Does not work for anyone.

Answers
1C 2A 3C 4B
5B 6C 7B 8A

Possible extended writing questions:
- Describe and evaluate biofeedback as a way of managing and coping with stress. *[AL = 16]*
- Discuss **two or more** ways of managing and coping with stress. *[AL = 16]*

Gender differences in coping with stress

Book-link

Y2/A Student Book
Pages 276–277

Y2/A Revision Guide
Pages 178–179

Spec Spotlight

Managing and
coping with stress:
gender differences in
coping with stress.

AO1

Males – tend to use problem-focused methods, root causes, direct, practical.

Females – tend to use emotion-focused methods, reduce anxiety of stressor.

Coping with infertility – men plan, women use avoidance (Peterson et al.).

Tend (protect) and befriend (seek support) is female response – adaptive for offspring (Taylor et al).

Oxytocin – hormone helps recovery from stress, drives tend and befriend in females.

Befriending is selective – usually only with other women, protect against males.

AO3

⊖ Misrepresents gender differences – different strategies due to different social roles.

⊖ Contradictory evidence – coping style depends on situation not gender (Porter and Stone).

⊖ No link – men and women use both methods depending on the stressor (Peterson et al.).

⊖ Retrospective research – depends on accurate recall of methods used in past.

⊕ Research support – for several predictions from tend and befriend (e.g Tamres et al.).

1 Problem-focused methods are linked to:
(a) Men and women.
(b) Women.
(c) Men.

2 Emotion-focused methods:
(a) Focus on reducing anxiety.
(b) Are more often used by men.
(c) Provide practical solutions.

3 Women use _____ to cope with stress.
(a) Fight or flight.
(b) Tend and befriend.
(c) Aggression.

4 The hormone that drives the female stress response is:
(a) Adrenaline.
(b) Testosterone.
(c) Oxytocin.

5 Men and women use different coping methods because they:
(a) Have different social roles.
(b) Are biologically different.
(c) Copy their same-sex parent.

6 Coping style appears to depend more on _____ than gender.
(a) Age.
(b) The situation.
(c) Personality.

7 Research that relies on accuracy of memory is:
(a) Retrospective.
(b) Prospective.
(c) Highly valid.

8 Tend and befriend is adaptive for:
(a) Individualistic cultures.
(b) Fathers and sons.
(c) Mothers and their offspring.

Answers 1C 2A 3B 4C 5A 6B 7A 8C

Possible extended writing questions:

- Outline and evaluate gender differences in coping with stress. *[AL = 16]*
- Discuss methods of managing and coping with stress. Refer to gender differences in your answer. *[AL = 16]*

Book-link

Y2/A Student Book
Pages 278–279

Y2/A Revision Guide
Pages 180–181

Spec Spotlight

Managing and coping with stress: the role of social support in coping with stress; types of social support, including instrumental, emotional and esteem support.

Instrumental support – practical and tangible (e.g. doing something).

Emotional support – not practical help, but aims to make person feel better, lift mood.

Esteem support – reinforce person's faith in their ability to cope, boost confidence.

All three interrelated – they overlap and can be given without physical presence.

Key study: Cohen et al.

Procedure – 404 adults, how many hugs received, exposed to cold virus.

Findings – more hugs/less illness, perceived social support buffered stress.

⊕ Research support – emotional support group better immune functioning (Fawzy et al.).

⊕ Benefits for women – use support more than men, live longer (Luckow).

⊖ Not always beneficial – when not sought out or 'wrong' type or from 'wrong' person.

⊖ Cultural differences – Asian-Americans less likely to seek support (Taylor et al.).

⊖ Depends on presence of stress – support offered when no stress is unwelcome.

1 Doing something practical to help is:
  (a) Emotional support.
  (b) Esteem support.
  (c) Instrumental support.

2 Giving esteem support involves:
  (a) Boosting someone's confidence.
  (b) Lifting someone's mood.
  (c) Helping someone practically.

3 All three types have in common:
  (a) Making someone feel better.
  (b) Can be given without being present.
  (c) Increasing faith in oneself.

4 Cohen *et al.* studied the stress-reducing effects of:
  (a) Drugs.
  (b) Hugs.
  (c) Bugs.

5 Being part of an emotional support group:
  (a) Reduces immune functioning.
  (b) Improves immune functioning.
  (c) Makes no difference at all.

6 Support is mostly beneficial when it is:
  (a) Provided by a close relative.
  (b) Given face-to-face.
  (c) Sought out by the recipient.

7 Which cultural group is less likely to seek social support?
  (a) Asian-Americans.
  (b) African-Americans.
  (c) European-Americans.

8 Support is usually welcome:
  (a) Only when the recipient is under stress.
  (b) In all circumstances.
  (c) When given by anyone at all.

Answers
1C 2A 3B 4B
5B 6C 7A 8A

Possible extended writing questions:
- Outline and evaluate the role of social support in coping with stress. *[AL = 16]*
- Discuss the roles of **two or more** types of social support in coping with stress. *[AL = 16]*

Neural and hormonal mechanisms in aggression

AO1   AO3

Topic 8: AGGRESSION

Neural mechanisms

Limbic system – speed and sensitivity predicts aggression in humans.

Amygdala – increased response leads to aggression (assess/respond to threats).

Serotonin – low levels disrupt orbitofrontal cortex, reduced self-control, aggression.

⊖ Not just limbic system – aggression also involves amygdala and reduced orbitofrontal cortex activity.

⊕ Research support – drugs that increase serotonin reduce aggression (Berman *et al.*).

⊖ Correlational research – neural links to aggression are complex.

Hormonal mechanisms

Testosterone – levels higher in men and linked to aggression.

Male prisoners – positive correlation between testosterone and aggression.

Animal studies – decreased testosterone leads to reduced aggression (castration).

⊕ Plausible mechanism – changes in testosterone levels after loss of status.

⊖ Mixed evidence – testosterone not involved when cortisol level is high.

⊖ Correlational research – hormonal links to aggression complex.

Spec Spotlight

Neural and hormonal mechanisms in aggression, including the roles of the limbic system, serotonin and testosterone.

Neural and hormonal mechanisms in aggression – multiple choice questions

1 Aggression is closely linked to sensitivity of the:
(a) Hypothalamus.
(b) Limbic system.
(c) Frontal cortex.

2 The part of the brain involved in assessing threats is the:
(a) Orbitofrontal cortex.
(b) Amygdala.
(c) Hypothalamus.

3 The hormone most closely linked to aggression is:
(a) Oestrogen.
(b) Cortisol.
(c) Testosterone.

4 Castration reduces testosterone and aggression in:
(a) Non-human animals.
(b) Females.
(c) Prisoners.

5 Aggression is *not* just linked to the limbic system but also to:
(a) Low testosterone levels.
(b) High serotonin levels.
(c) Reduced orbitofrontal cortex activity.

6 Aggression is reduced by drugs that:
(a) Increase serotonin.
(b) Decrease dopamine.
(c) Increase testosterone.

7 Testosterone does *not* influence aggression when:
(a) Serotonin level is low.
(b) Cortisol level is low.
(c) Cortisol level is high.

8 Neural and hormonal links to aggression are:
(a) Very well understood.
(b) Complex.
(c) Relatively trivial.

Answers
1B 2B 3C 4A
5C 6A 7C 8B

Possible extended writing questions:

- Outline and evaluate neural **and/or** hormonal mechanisms in aggression. *[AL = 16]*
- Discuss the roles of the limbic system, serotonin **and** testosterone in aggression. *[AL = 16]*

AO1

AO3

Book-link

Y2/A Student Book
Pages 292–293

Y2/A Revision Guide
Pages 184–185

Spec Spotlight

Genetic factors
in aggression, including
the MAOA gene.

Twin studies – genetic factors account for about 50% of variance in aggression.

Adoption studies – 41% of variance, Rhee and Waldman's meta-analysis.

MAOA gene (monoamine oxidase A) – gene for MAOA dysfunctional, low serotonin.

Warrior gene – low MAOA activity in brain, high aggression (Brunner *et al.*).

Violent domestic abuse – linked to low-activity MAOA gene (Stuart *et al.*).

MAOA gene – linked with aggression only when combined with early traumas.

⊖ Difficult to isolate genes – closely linked to environmental influences (e.g. cues).

⊖ Multiple influences – many genes interact with small effects, not single gene.

⊖ Measurement – findings depend on method, genes most influential when self-report used.

⊕ Research support – males with high-activity MAOA gene more prosocial (Martins *et al.*).

⊕ Support from animal studies – mice without MAOA gene hyper-aggressive (Goder *et al.*).

Topic 8: AGGRESSION

1 Genetic factors account for _____ of aggression in adoption studies.
(a) 76%
(b) 50%
(c) 41%

2 A dysfunctional MAOA gene is associated with:
(a) Low serotonin level.
(b) High serotonin level.
(c) Normal serotonin level.

3 The MAOA gene variant linked with aggression is nicknamed:
(a) Gladiator gene.
(b) Wrestler gene.
(c) Warrior gene.

4 MAOA gene is linked with aggression only when it:
(a) Is a high-activity variant.
(b) Is combined with early traumas.
(c) Occurs in twins.

5 It is very hard to isolate genes from the influence of:
(a) The environment.
(b) Innate factors.
(c) The weather.

6 Genetically, aggression is probably caused by:
(a) Many interacting genes.
(b) A single gene.
(c) A handful of key genes.

7 Genes appear influential when aggression is measured by:
(a) Direct observation.
(b) Self-report.
(c) Laboratory task.

8 Mice without the MAOA gene are:
(a) Withdrawn.
(b) Depressed.
(c) Hyper-aggressive.

Answers
1C 2A 3C 4B
5A 6A 7B 8C

Possible extended writing questions:

- Discuss genetic factors in aggression. *[AL = 16]*
- Describe and evaluate the MAOA gene in relation to genetic factors in aggression. *[AL = 16]*

A01

Ethological explanation of aggression

A03

Topic 8: AGGRESSION

Spec Spotlight

The ethological
explanation of
aggression, including
reference to innate
releasing mechanisms
and fixed action
patterns.

Aggression is adaptive – reduces competition, establishes dominance.

Aggression is ritualistic – set order ends with appeasement display (Lorenz).

Innate releasing mechanism – stimulus (e.g. face expression) activates IRM (e.g. brain circuit).

Fixed action pattern – IRM triggers FAP, ritualistic, universal, ballistic behaviour.

Key study: Tinbergen

Procedure – male sticklebacks saw wooden models.

Findings – sticklebacks only attacked models with red underside (stimulus activated IRM, IRM triggered FAP).

⊕ Research support – innate/genetic basis (low MAOA gene), amygdala is IRM (Brunner et al.).

⊖ Cultural differences – culture of honour in US south, learned social norm and not instinctive (Nisbett et al.).

⊖ Evidence against – ritualistic chimp slaughter not self-limiting (Goodall).

⊖ FAPs not fixed – influenced by learning and environment, flexible ('modal').

⊖ Generalisation – unjustified from birds and single species to complex human aggression.

Topic 8: AGGRESSION

1 Aggression is adaptive because it:
(a) Reduces competition.
(b) Establishes dominance.
(c) Both of the above.

2 According to Lorenz, most aggression ends in:
(a) Death.
(b) An appeasement display.
(c) Smiles and handshakes all round.

3 This is directly triggered by an environmental stimulus:
(a) An IRM.
(b) A FAP.
(c) Aggressive behaviour.

4 Tinbergen's sticklebacks only attacked models that:
(a) Were male.
(b) Looked like sticklebacks.
(c) Had a red underside.

5 Research supporting ethological theory shows that:
(a) Aggression is a learned social norm.
(b) There is an IRM in the amygdala.
(c) FAPs do not exist.

6 Cultural differences in aggression suggest that it is mostly:
(a) Innate.
(b) Learned.
(c) Universal.

7 Goodall found that chimp aggression was:
(a) Not self-limiting.
(b) Ended by appeasement.
(c) Not ritualistic.

8 A more accepted term for fixed action pattern is:
(a) Modal action pattern.
(b) Flexible action pattern.
(c) Inflexible action pattern.

Answers
1C 2B 3A 4C
5B 6B 7A 8A

Possible extended writing questions:

- Outline and evaluate the ethological explanation of aggression. *[AL = 16]*
- Discuss the ethological explanation of aggression. Refer in your answer to innate releasing mechanisms **and** fixed actions patterns. *[AL = 16]*

Evolutionary explanations of human aggression

Book-link

Y2/A Student Book
Pages 296–297

Y2/A Revision Guide
Pages 188–189

Spec Spotlight

Evolutionary explanations of human aggression.

AO1

Mate retention strategies – adaptive for males because avoids cuckoldry (so more reproductively successful).

For example – direct guarding (checking partner), negative inducements (threats).

Physical violence against partner – more likely in men using these strategies.

Bullying – adaptive because increases own health and reproductive chances.

Male bullying – ensures access to females and reduces threats from other males.

Female bullying – secures partner's fidelity and resources for offspring.

AO3

(+) Research support – retention strategies are linked with sexual jealousy and aggression (e.g. Shackelford et al.).

(+) Explains gender differences – females less aggressive, risks to offspring.

(+) Real-life application – could make anti-bullying interventions more effective.

(−) Cultural differences – little aggression in some cultures (!Kung San), so not universal/innate.

(−) Methodological issues – research correlational so no cause-and-effect.

1 Mate retention strategies are adaptive for males because they:
(a) Reduce sexual jealousy.
(b) Avoid risk of cuckoldry.
(c) Reduce aggression.

2 Monitoring your partner's behaviour is an example of:
(a) Physical violence.
(b) Negative inducements.
(c) Direct guarding.

3 Male bullying is adaptive because it:
(a) Ensures access to females.
(b) Increases competition from other males.
(c) Reduces reproductive success.

4 Female bullying:
(a) Is not adaptive for the female.
(b) Secures a partner's fidelity.
(c) Guarantees access to males.

5 Men using mate retention strategies are more likely to use:
(a) Physical violence.
(b) Non-physical violence.
(c) Hand gestures.

6 Females are less aggressive than males because:
(a) Aggression is risky for offspring.
(b) They are physically weaker.
(c) Aggression is not adaptive for females.

7 Cultural differences show that aggression is mostly:
(a) Innate.
(b) Learned.
(c) Instinctive.

8 Correlational research allows us to conclude that aggression:
(a) Is fully explained by evolution.
(b) Is caused by adaptive factors.
(c) Is linked to adaptive factors.

Answers
1B 2C 3A 4B
5A 6A 7B 8C

Possible extended writing questions:

- Discuss evolutionary **and/or** ethological explanations of human aggression. *[AL = 16]*
- Outline and evaluate evolutionary explanations of human aggression. *[AL = 16]*

Social-psychological explanations: Frustration-aggression hypothesis

Book-link

Y2/A Student Book
Pages 298–299

Y2/A Revision Guide
Pages 190–191

Spec Spotlight

Social psychological explanations of human aggression, including the frustration-aggression hypothesis.

AO1

Dollard *et al.* – frustration always leads to aggression, aggression is always the result of frustration.

Catharsis – aggression is a drive, reduced by expressing it ('get it off your chest').

Indirect – aggression may be displaced because cause of frustration is abstract, powerful or unavailable.

Weapons effect – frustration creates readiness, cues trigger aggression.

Key study: Geen

Procedure – students' levels of frustration manipulated during jigsaw puzzle.

Findings – all frustrated students gave bigger shocks than control group.

AO3

⊕ Research evidence – displaced aggression is a reliable finding (meta-analysis, Marcus-Newhall *et al.*).

⊖ Not cathartic – venting anger results in more aggression not less (Bushman).

⊕ Reformulated hypothesis – aggression triggered by negative feelings generally (Berkowitz).

⊖ Justified versus unjustified – unjustified frustration produces more aggression.

⊕ Real-life application – informs gun control debate ('trigger pulls the finger').

Social-psychological explanations. Frustration aggression hypothesis – *multiple choice questions*

1 Aggressive behaviour is cathartic because aggression is:
(a) Learned.
(b) A social norm.
(c) A drive.

2 Aggression is:
(a) Always directed at the cause of frustration.
(b) Sometimes indirect.
(c) Not related to frustration.

3 The weapons effect illustrates the importance of:
(a) Catharsis.
(b) Cues.
(c) Displaced aggression.

4 In Geen's study, the biggest shocks were given by the:
(a) Least frustrated students.
(b) Control group.
(c) Most frustrated students.

5 Research evidence shows that displaced aggression:
(a) Is a reliable finding.
(b) Does not exist.
(c) Causes frustration.

6 Bushman found that:
(a) Aggression is cathartic.
(b) Venting anger creates more aggression.
(c) 'The trigger pulls the finger.'

7 According to the reformulated hypothesis, aggression:
(a) Is triggered by negative feelings generally.
(b) Is not a drive.
(c) Is always the result of frustration.

8 Aggression is greater when the frustration is:
(a) Moderate.
(b) Justified.
(c) Unjustified.

Topic 8: AGGRESSION

Answers
1C 2B 3B 4C
5A 6B 7A 8C

Possible extended writing questions:

- Discuss **one** social-psychological explanation of aggression. *[AL = 16]*
- Describe and evaluate the frustration-aggression hypothesis as an explanation of aggression. *[AL = 16]*

AO1   AO3

Topic 8: AGGRESSION

Book-link

Y2/A Student Book
Pages 300–301

Y2/A Revision Guide
Pages 192–193

Spec Spotlight

Social psychological explanations of aggression, including social learning theory as applied to human aggression.

Aggression can be learned directly – positive and negative reinforcement.

Most aggression learned indirectly – observation and vicarious reinforcement.

Social learning requires attention, retention, reproduction and motivation.

Self-efficacy – increases each time child learns that aggression brings valued rewards.

Key study: Bandura et al.

Procedure – children observed model play with toys, including 'bobo doll'.

Findings – children who observed aggression behaved aggressively towards the doll (imitation).

⊕ Supportive evidence – aggressive boys become friends, models for each other (Poulin and Boivin).

⊖ Cannot explain all aggression – e.g. reactive (hot-blooded, angry).

⊕ Seek non-aggressive models – friends for children to imitate.

⊕ Real-life application – media could show non-aggression being rewarded.

⊖ Cultural differences – some cultures have no aggressive models, but still aggression, e.g. !Kung San.

Topic 8: AGGRESSION

1 Positive reinforcement is an example of _____ learning.
(a) Indirect.
(b) Direct.
(c) Vicarious.

2 Most reinforcement in social learning of aggression is:
(a) Positive.
(b) Vicarious.
(c) Negative.

3 Two requirements of social learning are:
(a) Retention and detention.
(b) Motivation and registration.
(c) Attention and reproduction.

4 Bandura *et al.* found that _____ was a powerful form of learning.
(a) Imitation.
(b) Classical conditioning.
(c) Operant conditioning.

5 When aggressive children become friends, they:
(a) Restrain each other's aggression.
(b) Spend little time together.
(c) Provide models for each other to imitate.

6 SLT has difficulty explaining:
(a) Hot-blooded aggression.
(b) Cold-blooded aggression.
(c) Calculating, goal-directed aggression.

7 SLT can be applied to:
(a) Media portrayals of aggression.
(b) Hormonal mechanisms in aggression.
(c) Genetics of aggression.

8 Self-efficacy increases each time:
(a) A bobo doll is hit.
(b) A child sees that aggression is a valued resource.
(c) There is reactive violence.

Answers
1B 2B 3C 4A
5C 6A 7A 8B

Possible extended writing questions:
- Outline and evaluate **two** social-psychological explanations of aggression. *[AL = 16]*
- Discuss social learning theory as an explanation of human aggression. *[AL = 16]*

AO1

Social-psychological explanations: De-individuation

AO3

Reduced personal responsibility –
de-individuation in a crowd, ignore social
norms (Zimbardo).

Anonymity – promotes de-individuation and
aggression, no fear of retribution.

Anonymity – reduces private self-awareness,
think less about feelings.

Anonymity – reduces public self-awareness,
don't care how others see us.

Key study: Dodd

Procedure – students indicated what they
would do if they could never be identified.

Findings – 36% responses antisocial, 26%
criminal acts, only 9% prosocial.

(+) Supportive evidence – correlation
between anonymity and hostility online
(Douglas and McGarty).

(−) Contradictory evidence – anonymity did
not lead to aggression in Gergen et al.

(−) Aggression not inevitable –
de-individuation can lead to prosocial
behaviour.

(+) Real-life application – e.g. help
understand/reduce aggression online.

(−) Alternative explanation – SIDE model,
behaviour conforms to local norms
(Spears and Lee).

Topic 8: AGGRESSION

Spec Spotlight

Social
psychological
explanations of human
aggression, including
de-individuation.

1 When in a crowd, we may:
(a) Fear that we stand out.
(b) Lose a sense of responsibility.
(c) Become aware of our feelings.

2 A major promotor of de-individuation is:
(a) Knowing lots of people.
(b) An unusual hairstyle.
(c) Anonymity.

3 Reduced public self-awareness means we:
(a) Don't monitor our own behaviour.
(b) Think deeply about our feelings.
(c) Don't care how others view us.

4 In Dodd's study, what percentage of responses were actual criminal acts?
(a) 9%
(b) 26%
(c) 36%

5 The relationship between online anonymity and hostility is:
(a) A negative correlation.
(b) A positive correlation.
(c) Cause-and-effect.

6 Gergen *et al.* found that anonymity:
(a) Did not lead to aggression.
(b) Caused aggression.
(c) Was not related to crowd behaviour.

7 De-individuation:
(a) Always leads to aggression.
(b) Does not exist online.
(c) Can lead to prosocial behaviour.

8 An alternative explanation of de-individuation is the:
(a) SIDE model.
(b) FRONT model.
(c) BACK model.

Answers 1B 2C 3C 4B 5B 6A 7C 8A

Possible extended writing questions:
- Discuss **one** social-psychological explanation and **one other** explanation of aggression. *[AL = 16]*
- Describe and evaluate de-individuation as an explanation of human aggression. *[AL = 16]*

| AO1 | Institutional aggression in the context of prisons | AO3 |

Spec Spotlight

Institutional aggression in the context of prisons: dispositional and situational explanations.

Dispositional explanation

Importation model – traits of prisoners, aggressive subculture imported into prison (Irwin and Cressey).

Characteristics include anger, traumatic experiences, history of violence.

Outcomes – include aggression, self-harm, compared with control group (DeLisi *et al.*).

(+) Research support – characteristics of inmates more important than prison environment (Camp and Gaes).

(−) Better alternative – poorly managed prisons more likely to have violence (Dilulio).

Situational explanation

Deprivation model – harsh prison conditions cause stress and aggression (Clemmer).

Deprivation – physical (lack of goods) and psychological (lack of freedom).

Prison-level factors – e.g. use of protective custody, predict inmate violence (Steiner).

(+) Research support – inmate homicides motivated by prison deprivations (Cunningham *et al.*).

(−) Contradictory evidence – conjugal visits do not reduce aggression (Hensley *et al.*).

(−) Interactionist model – prison features and individual characteristics combined.

Institutional aggression in the context of prisons – *multiple choice questions*

1 An example of a dispositional theory of prison aggression is:
(a) Social learning theory.
(b) The deprivation model.
(c) The importation model.

2 The importation model claims a main cause of aggression is:
(a) How a prison is run.
(b) Prisoners' characteristics.
(c) Features of the situation.

3 Deprivation can lead to aggression because it may cause:
(a) Aggressive personality traits.
(b) Stress.
(c) Childhood trauma.

4 Deprivation in prison leading to aggression can be:
(a) Physical.
(b) Psychological.
(c) Both of the above.

5 Camp and Gaes found that:
(a) Inmate characteristics are central to aggression.
(b) Dispositional theory is wrong.
(c) The deprivation model is right.

6 There is more violence in:
(a) Well-run prisons.
(b) Poorly managed prisons.
(c) Smaller prisons.

7 Research into conjugal visits shows that:
(a) Most prisoners are aggressive.
(b) The deprivation model is valid.
(c) Aggression is not reduced.

8 The _____ combines individual and prison characteristics.
(a) Interactionist model.
(b) Importation model.
(c) Deprivation theory.

Answers
1C 2B 3B 4C
5A 6B 7C 8A

Possible extended writing questions:

- Discuss institutional aggression in the context of prisons. *[AL = 16]*
- Outline and evaluate **one** dispositional **and** one situational explanation of institutional aggression in the context of prisons. *[AL = 16]*

Media influences: Effects of computer games

Book-link

Y2/A Student Book
Pages 306–307

Y2/A Revision Guide
Pages 198–199

Spec Spotlight

Media influences on aggression, including the effects of computer games.

AO1

Experiment – violent games cause greater aggression in laboratory tasks (Bartholow and Anderson).

Correlation – positive correlation between aggression and violent game-playing in juvenile offenders (DeLisi et al.).

Longitudinal – time watching TV as child is reliable predictor of aggression as adult (Robertson et al.).

Meta-analysis – link between games and aggression, both genders and across cultures (Anderson et al.).

Effects of violent game-playing on aggression – greater than effect of smoke on cancer (Anderson et al.).

AO3

⊕ Artificial measures – unrealistic lab tasks, plus no chance of retaliation.

⊕ Non-equivalence problem – violent and non-violent games not comparable.

⊖ No cause-and-effect – correlation may be because violent people choose violent games.

⊕ Confounding variables – longitudinal studies, many factors interact over time.

⊖ Publication bias – non-significant findings not published, affects meta-analyses.

Topic 8: AGGRESSION

1 A common methodology for studying effects of computer games is:
(a) Interviews.
(b) Observational studies.
(c) Meta-analysis.

2 The correlation between aggression and game-playing is:
(a) Negative.
(b) Positive.
(c) Zero.

3 A reliable media-linked predictor of aggression in adulthood is:
(a) Time watching TV as an adult.
(b) Time watching TV as a child.
(c) Aggression in childhood.

4 Anderson *et al.* compared effects of games on aggression with:
(a) Effects of smoking on cancer.
(b) The link between diet and obesity.
(c) The effects of stress on illness.

5 Lab experiments are limited because:
(a) Variables are not controlled.
(b) Aggression measures are artificial.
(c) Can't establish cause-and-effect.

6 'Violent and non-violent games cannot be compared' is the:
(a) Non-equivalence problem.
(b) Non-equine problem.
(c) Non-equidistant problem.

7 Confounding variables are a particular problem in:
(a) Laboratory experiments.
(b) Meta-analysis.
(c) Longitudinal studies.

8 Aggression-media link may be exaggerated because of:
(a) A lack of cause and effect.
(b) Publication bias.
(c) Extraneous variables.

Answers
1C 2B 3B 4A
5B 6A 7C 8B

Possible extended writing questions:
- Describe and evaluate research into media influences on aggression. *[AL = 16]*
- Discuss the effects of computer games on aggression. *[AL = 16]*

Book-link

Y2/A Student Book
Pages 308–309

Y2/A Revision Guide
Pages 200–201

Spec Spotlight

Media influences on aggression. The role of desensitisation, disinhibition and cognitive priming.

Media influences on aggression

AO1

AO3

Desensitisation

Reduced physiological response to media violence (less arousal).

Also reduced psychological response – e.g. less empathy for victims of violence.

⊕ Research support – lower arousal in habitual viewers of violent media (Krahé *et al.*).

⊖ Better explanation – catharsis, viewing violent media releases aggression.

Disinhibition

Exposure to violent media loosens restraints against aggression.

Enhanced if aggression in media rewarded – changed social norms.

⊕ Research support – film showed aggression as vengeance, more shocks given (Berkowitz and Alioto).

⊕ Explains effects of cartoon violence – children learn social norms.

Cognitive priming

Media gives 'script' to follow in response to aggressive cues.

Songs with aggressive lyrics – act as cues, may trigger violent attitudes and behaviours.

⊕ Real-life application of priming – interventions challenge aggressive cognitive scripts.

1 A reduced physiological response to violent media is part of:
(a) Desensitisation.
(b) Disinhibition.
(c) Cognitive priming.

2 Seeing aggression rewarded in media enhances:
(a) Desensitisation.
(b) Disinhibition.
(c) Cognitive priming.

3 Cognitive priming claims media provides us with:
(a) An aggressive 'script' to follow.
(b) Aggressive models to imitate.
(c) Operant conditioning.

4 Aggressive cues can trigger:
(a) Aggressive attitudes.
(b) Violent behaviours.
(c) Both of the above.

5 Habitual viewers of media violence show arousal levels that are:
(a) Higher.
(b) Lower.
(c) Wider.

6 'Viewing violent media releases aggressive impulses' is:
(a) Catharsis.
(b) Social learning.
(c) Vicarious reinforcement.

7 Removal of constraints against violence in media supports:
(a) Desensitisation theory.
(b) Cognitive priming.
(c) Disinhibition theory.

8 Interventions based on cognitive priming:
(a) Provide non-aggressive models.
(b) Use drugs to reduce aggression.
(c) Challenge aggressive scripts.

Answers
1A 2B 3A 4C
5B 6A 7C 8C

Possible extended writing questions:

- Outline and evaluate research into **two or more** media influences on aggression. *[AL = 16]*
- In relation to media influences on aggression, discuss the roles of desensitisation, disinhibition **and** cognitive priming. *[AL = 16]*

Book-link

Y2/A Student Book
Pages 320–321

Y2/A Revision Guide
Pages 202–203

Spec Spotlight

Problems in
defining crime.
Ways of measuring
crime, including official
statistics, victim surveys
and offender surveys.

AO1 — Defining and measuring crime

Crime – any act that breaks the law and warrants some form of punishment.

Definitions differ across cultures – e.g. forced marriage.

Definitions differ across different historical times – e.g. homosexuality.

Official statistics – government record of total number of crimes reported and recorded by the police.

Victim surveys – record of people's experience of crime in a specific period, CSEW involves 50,000 households.

Offender surveys – people volunteer details of crimes they have committed.

AO3

⊖ Official statistics may underestimate crime – 75% of crime = the 'dark figure'.

⊕ Victim surveys are more accurate – include unreported crime.

⊕ Offender surveys provide insight – on how many people are responsible though issues with sampling.

⊖ The politics of measuring crime – validity of official statistics (ONS) questioned.

⊕ A multidisciplinary approach – combine all methods for best insight.

1 Not an issue with defining crime:
(a) History.
(b) Culture.
(c) Gender.

2 Total number of crimes reported and recorded by the police:
(a) Victim surveys.
(b) Official statistics.
(c) Offender surveys.

3 Households involved in the CSEW (Crime Survey for England in Wales):
(a) 50,000.
(b) 75,000.
(c) 100,000.

4 A strength of offender surveys:
(a) Representative sample.
(b) Insight into numbers responsible.
(c) Responses are highly reliable.

5 ONS stands for:
(a) Office of Northwest Surveys.
(b) Office of Numerical Systems.
(c) Office of National Statistics.

6 People volunteer details of their crimes:
(a) Victim surveys.
(b) Offender surveys.
(c) Official statistics.

7 The dark figure is estimated to include:
(a) 25% of crime.
(b) 50% of crime.
(c) 75% of crime.

8 Likely to include unreported crime:
(a) Victim surveys.
(b) Offender surveys.
(c) Official statistics.

Answers
1C 2B 3A 4B
5C 6B 7C 8A

Possible extended writing questions:
- Explain **two** problems in defining crime. [AL = 6]
- Outline and evaluate ways of measuring crime. [AL = 16]

Book-link

Y2/A Student Book
Pages 322–323

Y2/A Revision Guide
Pages 204–205

Spec Spotlight

Offender profiling: the top-down approach, including organised and disorganised types of offender.

Offender profiling: The top-down approach

A01

Offender profiling – aims to narrow list of suspects using crime scene evidence.

Top-down approach – match crime / offender to pre-existing templates.

Organised and disorganised types – based on offenders' 'ways of working'.

Organised – planned, targets victim, high IQ, high control, married, skilled job.

Disorganised – no planning, impulsive, lower IQ, lives alone, unskilled job.

FBI profile – data assimilation → crime scene classification → crime reconstruction → profile generation.

A03

⊖ Only applies to particular crimes – e.g. rape, arson, murder, not burglary.

⊖ Based on outdated models of personality – poor validity (Alison et al.).

⊖ Little evidence of disorganised type – from smallest space analysis (Canter et al.).

⊖ Classification system is too simplistic – e.g. more types of serial killer (Holmes).

⊖ Poor methods to develop typology – interviews with only 36 US killers.

1 *Not* a type associated with the top-down approach:
- (a) Organised.
- (b) Unorganised.
- (c) Disorganised.

2 *Not* a feature of organised offenders:
- (a) Lack of planning.
- (b) High IQ.
- (c) Targets victim.

3 Associated with disorganised offenders:
- (a) Impulsive.
- (b) Tend to be married/in a relationship.
- (c) Offender has a 'type'.

4 *Not* part of FBI profile generation:
- (a) Data assimilation.
- (b) Deconstruction.
- (c) Profile generation.

5 Crime that does *not* suit the top-down approach.
- (a) Arson.
- (b) Rape.
- (c) Burglary.

6 Found little evidence for disorganised type:
- (a) Canter *et al.*
- (b) Alison *et al.*
- (c) Holmes *et al.*

7 Number of serial killers who were interviewed to develop approach:
- (a) 36
- (b) 46
- (c) 56

8 Matching crime/offender to existing templates:
- (a) Top-up approach.
- (b) Top-down approach.
- (c) Top-side approach.

Answers
1B 2A 3A 4B
5C 6A 7A 8B

Possible extended writing questions:
- Outline and evaluate the top-down approach to offender profiling. *[AL = 16]*
- Discuss organised and disorganised types of offender. *[AL = 16]*

Offender profiling: The bottom-up approach

AO1

Book-link

Y2/A Student Book
Pages 324–325

Y2/A Revision Guide
Pages 206–207

Spec Spotlight

Offender profiling:
the bottom-up
approach, including
investigative
psychology;
geographical
profiling.

Investigative psychology

Bottom up approach – profile is data-driven, emerges as offence is studied.

Statistical analysis – detect patterns across offences, using crime-scene evidence.

Interpersonal coherence – way offender behaves at the scene reflects their life.

Geographical profiling

Inferences about offender's base from locations of crime.

Marauder and commuter – crime close to home base or travel distance from home.

Circle theory – offences form a circle around offender's home base.

AO3

(+) Evidence for investigative psychology – content analysis of 66 sexual assault cases (Canter and Heritage).

(+) Evidence for geographical profiling – 120 US serial killer cases (Lundrigan and Canter).

(+) Scientific basis – use of geographical, biological and psychological data.

(+) Wider application – smallest space analysis can be used for burglary.

(−) Mixed results for profiling – 48 police forces, useful in 8% of cases (Copson).

1 *Not* a form of bottom-up profiling:
- (a) Geographical approach.
- (b) Typology approach.
- (c) Investigative approach.

2 The way the offender behaves at the scenes reflects their daily life:
- (a) Interpersonal coherence.
- (b) Individual concordance.
- (c) Personal correspondence.

3 Operates close to their home base:
- (a) Maverick.
- (b) Menace.
- (c) Marauder.

4 Technique used in investigative psychology:
- (a) Smallest space analysis.
- (b) Micro-scene analysis.
- (c) Statistical crime analysis.

5 Number of successful identifications in Copson's study:
- (a) 6%.
- (b) 8%.
- (c) 10%.

6 Unlike the top-down approach, the bottom-up model can be applied to:
- (a) Murder.
- (b) Arson
- (c) Burglary.

7 Found evidence for geographical profiling:
- (a) Lundrigan and Canter.
- (b) Canter and Heritage.
- (c) Heritage and Lundrigan.

8 Part of geographical profiling:
- (a) Square theory.
- (b) Triangle theory.
- (c) Circle theory.

Answers 1B 2A 3C 4A 5B 6C 7A 8C

Topic 9: FORENSIC PSYCHOLOGY

Possible extended writing questions:
- Discuss the bottom-up approach to offender profiling. *[AL = 16]*
- Outline and evaluate **two** approaches to offender profiling. *[AL = 16]*

Book-link

Y2/A Student Book
Pages 326–327

Y2/A Revision Guide
Pages 208–209

Spec Spotlight

Biological explanations of offending behaviour: an historical approach (atavistic form).

AO1

Lombroso – 19th C, criminals are genetic throwbacks, primitive sub-species.

Offenders lack evolutionary development – cannot adjust to civilised society.

Biologically determined – features of the head and face that make them different.

Cranial and emotional features – sloping brow, prominent jaw, insensitive to pain.

Different crimes associated with different characteristics – murderer = curly hair.

Lombroso research – 383 dead and 3839 live criminals, 40% of criminal acts accounted for by atavistic characteristics.

AO3

⊕ Large contribution – shift from moralistic to scientific, father of modern criminology (Hollin).

⊖ Racial undertones of Lombroso's work – many atavistic features are African.

⊖ Contradictory evidence – no physical differences for offenders and non-offenders (Goring).

⊖ Poor control in Lombroso's research – no non-criminal control group (Goring used controls).

⊖ Causation is a problem in Lombroso's theory – other factors matter, e.g. poverty.

Topic 9: FORENSIC PSYCHOLOGY

1 Proposed the atavistic form:
(a) Lombroso.
(b) Lobrosso.
(c) Lomberto.

2 Atavism suggests that criminals are:
(a) Made and not born.
(b) Found only in primitive cultures.
(c) Primitive sub-species.

3 An atavistic feature of murderers:
(a) Curly hair.
(b) Blonde hair.
(c) No hair.

4 A feature of atavism:
(a) Prominent brow.
(b) Receding jaw.
(c) Insensitive to pain.

5 Percentage of Lombroso's sample that were atavistic:
(a) 34%
(b) 37%
(c) 40%

6 Weakness of Lombroso's work:
(a) Small samples studied.
(b) No lasting influence.
(c) Racial undertones.

7 Positive contribution of Lombroso's work:
(a) Moralistic emphasis
(b) Scientific emphasis.
(c) Control group.

8 Found no physical differences between offenders and non-offenders:
(a) Boring.
(b) Goring.
(c) Hollin.

Possible extended writing questions:
- Describe and evaluate the atavistic form. *[AL = 16]*
- Discuss **one** biological explanation of offending. *[AL = 16]*

Book-link

Y2/A Student Book
Pages 328–329

Y2/A Revision Guide
Pages 210–211

Spec Spotlight

Biological
explanations of
offending behaviour:
genetics and neural
explanations.

AO1 Biological explanations. Genetic and neural explanations **AO3**

Genetic explanation

Twin and adoption studies suggest criminal predisposition.

Candidate genes – MAOA and CDH13 found in 900 offenders (Tiihonen *et al.*).

Diathesis-stress model = genes + stressor/ trigger (e.g. upbringing).

Neural explanation

Neural differences in people with APD.

Prefrontal cortex – 11% less grey matter (Raine *et al.*), less emotional regulation.

Mirror neurons (empathy) – de-activated by a neural switch in the criminal brain.

⊖ Methodological problems with twin studies – poor control of environment.

⊕ Support for diathesis-stress – Danish adoption study (Mednick *et al.*).

⊖ Methodological problems of twin studies – late adoption, regular contact.

⊖ Biological reductionism – ignores poverty, deprivation, mental illness.

⊖ Biological determinism – criminal gene presents a problem for legal system.

1 *Not* typically used to investigate genetic links in crime:
(a) Adoption studies.
(b) Animal studies.
(c) Twin studies.

2 *Not* a candidate gene linked to offending:
(a) MAOA.
(b) MDH.
(c) CDH13.

3 Genes + trigger = offending:
(a) Dimorphic-stress model.
(b) Dizygotic-stress model.
(c) Diathesis-stress model.

4 APD stands for:
(a) Adult psychopathy disorder.
(b) Antisocial personality disorder.
(c) Affectionless person disorder.

5 May activate empathy in the brain:
(a) Mirror neurons.
(b) Motor neurons.
(c) Mediating neurons.

6 Mednick *et al.*'s adoption study took place in:
(a) Finland.
(b) Scotland.
(c) Denmark.

7 The idea of the criminal gene:
(a) Presents a problem for the legal system.
(b) Cannot be explained by diathesis-stress.
(c) Is well-supported by research.

8 Percentage reduction of grey matter in Raine *et al.*'s study:
(a) 9
(b) 11
(c) 13

Topic 9: FORENSIC PSYCHOLOGY

Answers
1B 2B 3C 4B
5A 6C 7A 8B

Possible extended writing questions:

- Discuss genetic **and/or** neural explanations of offending. *[AL = 16]*
- Outline and evaluate **two or more** biological explanations of offending. *[AL = 16]*

Psychological explanations: Eysenck's theory

Book-link

Y2/A Student Book
Pages 330–331

Y2/A Revision Guide
Pages 212–213

Spec Spotlight

Psychological
explanations of
offending behaviour:
Eysenck's theory of the
criminal personality.

AO1

Three personality dimensions – introversion-extraversion, neuroticism-stability, psychoticism-stability.

Innate, biological basis – e.g. E have underactive nervous system, N have reactive sympathetic nervous system.

Criminal personality = neurotic (N) + extravert (E) + high psychoticism (P).

Criminal behaviour – selfish, immediate gratification, developmentally immature.

High E and N scorers – lack ability to learn (be conditioned).

Personality – measured using Eysenck Personality Inventory (EPI), P added later.

AO3

⊕ Research support – prisoners high on E, P and N scores (Farrington et al.).

⊖ More than one single criminal type – add openness, conscientiousness agreeableness (Digman).

⊖ Cultural bias – Hispanic/African-American offenders low E (Bartol and Holanchock).

⊖ Mismeasurement of personality – can't reduce personality to a score.

⊕ Theory fits with biological approaches – e.g. Raine's work on APD and brain structure.

Psychological explanations: Eysenck's theory – multiple choice questions

1 N-S as a dimension of personality stands for:
(a) Neuroticism-stability.
(b) Neuroticism -sociability.
(c) Nervousness-solidity.

2 Personality type is based on our inherited:
(a) Nervous system.
(b) Social system.
(c) Cognitive system.

3 Feature of the criminal type:
(a) Unselfishness.
(b) Developmentally immature.
(c) Delayed gratification.

4 Eysenck's criminal type:
(a) I, N + S.
(b) E, N + P.
(c) E, S + P.

5 EPI stands for:
(a) Eysenck's people index.
(b) Eysenck's personality inventory.
(c) Eysenck's psychological indicators.

6 Digman criticised Eysenck by proposing adding:
(a) Friendliness.
(b) Warmth.
(c) Openness.

7 Found evidence in support of Eysenck's theory:
(a) Farrington et al.
(b) Fotherham et al.
(c) Furlington et al.

8 Eysenck's theory supports Raine's work on:
(a) Hormonal imbalance.
(b) Brain structure.
(c) Chromosomal abnormality.

Answers
1A 2A 3C 4B
5B 6C 7A 8B

Possible extended writing questions:

- Discuss **one** psychological and **one** biological explanation of offending behaviour. *[AL = 16]*
- Describe and evaluate Eysenck's theory of the criminal behaviour. *[AL = 16]*

Book-link

Y2/A Student Book
Pages 332–333

Y2/A Revision Guide
Pages 214–215

Psychological explanations: Cognitive explanations

A01

Level of moral reasoning

Higher the stage the more sophisticated reasoning (Kohlberg).

Criminals at preconventional level – avoid punishment, gain rewards.

Offenders more egocentric and show less empathy – poor perspective-taking.

Cognitive distortions

Faulty and biased thinking helps criminals justify behaviour.

Hostile attribution bias – perceive non-aggressive cues as confrontational.

Minimalisation – downplay significance of a crime, reduces sense of guilt.

A03

⊕ Research support – less mature moral reasoning in offenders (Palmer and Hollin).

⊖ Better theories of moral reasoning – mature–immature reasoning (Gibbs).

⊕ Real-life application of cognitive distortions – use of CBT to reduce faulty thinking.

⊖ Individual differences in levels of reasoning – often depends on crime, e.g. robbery versus assault.

⊖ Cognitive explanations are descriptive, not explanatory – 'after the fact'.

Spec Spotlight

Psychological explanations of offending behaviour: cognitive explanations; level of moral reasoning and cognitive distortions, including hostile attribution bias and minimalisation.

1 Levels of moral reasoning was proposed by:
(a) Karlberg.
(b) Kleinberg.
(c) Kohlberg.

2 Criminals are at the:
(a) Preconventional level.
(b) Conventional level.
(c) Postconventional level.

3 Characteristic of criminal reasoning:
(a) Less egocentric.
(b) Poor perspective-taking.
(c) More empathic.

4 A type of cognitive distortion:
(a) Hostile argumentative bias.
(b) Hostile application bias.
(c) Hostile attribution bias.

5 Downplaying the significance of a crime:
(a) Minimalisation.
(b) Simplification.
(c) Over-generalisation.

6 Found evidence to support levels of moral reasoning:
(a) Potter and Harris.
(b) Perkins and Henry.
(c) Palmer and Hollin.

7 Cognitive distortion research has proved useful in:
(a) TBC.
(b) CBT.
(c) CTB.

8 Cognitive explanations tend to be:
(a) Explanatory not descriptive.
(b) Descriptive not explanatory.
(c) Both descriptive and explanatory.

Answers
1C 2A 3B 4C
5A 6C 7B 8B

Possible extended writing questions:

- Outline and evaluate cognitive explanations of offending behaviour. *[AL = 16]*
- Discuss level of moral reasoning **and** cognitive distortions as explanations of offending behaviour. *[AL = 16]*

Book-link

Y2/A Student Book
Pages 334–335

Y2/A Revision Guide
Pages 216–217

Spec Spotlight

Psychological explanations of offending behaviour: differential association theory.

Psychological explanations: Differential association

AO1

Set of scientific principles to explain all types of offending (Sutherland).

Crime is learned – through interactions with significant others.

Crime occurs if exposure to pro-crime attitudes outweighs anti-crime attitudes.

Mathematical prediction – based on frequency, intensity, duration of exposure.

Techniques and attitudes learned – e.g. how to break into a car.

Reoffending due to socialisation in prison – learning pro-crime attitudes.

AO3

⊕ Explanatory power – can account for crime in all sectors of society.

⊕ Contribution to criminology – highlights dysfunctional social circumstances.

⊖ Difficult to test – how can pro- and anti-crime attitudes be measured?

⊖ Alternative explanations – crime running in families could be genetic.

⊖ Determinist explanation – stereotypes not everyone from poor backgrounds becomes criminal.

Psychological explanations. Differential association – *multiple choice questions*

1 Proposed differential association:
 (a) Sunderland.
 (b) Sutherland.
 (c) Southland.

2 *Not* required to mathematically predict crime:
 (a) Frequency of pro-crime attitudes.
 (b) Duration of pro-crime attitudes.
 (c) Variability of pro-crime attitudes.

3 For crime to occur:
 (a) Pro-crime < anti-crime attitudes.
 (b) Pro-crime > anti-crime attitudes.
 (c) Pro-crime = anti-crime attitudes.

4 Socialisation in prison may explain:
 (a) Reoffending.
 (b) Retribution.
 (c) Rehabilitation.

5 Differential association consists of:
 (a) Subjective principles.
 (b) Scientific principles.
 (c) Criminal strategies.

6 *Not* a strength of differential association:
 (a) Straightforward to test.
 (b) Can account for many crimes.
 (c) Contribution to criminology.

7 Crime running in families could also be explained by:
 (a) Cognition.
 (b) Personality.
 (c) Genetics.

8 Stereotyping people from poor backgrounds may be an issue of:
 (a) Reductionism.
 (b) Determinism.
 (c) Holism.

Answers
1B 2C 3B 4A
5B 6A 7C 8B

Topic 9: FORENSIC PSYCHOLOGY

Possible extended writing questions:

- Discuss **one or more** psychological explanations of offending behaviour. *[AL = 16]*
- Outline and evaluate differential association theory. *[AL = 16]*

Book-link

Y2/A Student Book
Pages 336–337

Y2/A Revision Guide
Pages 218–219

Spec Spotlight

Psychological explanations of offending behaviour: psychodynamic explanations.

Inadequate superego – can lead to offending, three types (Blackburn).

(1) Weak superego – absence of same-sex parent, no identification in phallic stage.

(2) Deviant superego – same-sex parent has criminal attitudes, are internalised.

(3) Over-harsh superego – unconscious drive to satisfy need for punishment.

Loss of attachment – leads to affectionless psychopathy and delinquency (Bowlby).

44 juvenile thieves study – prolonged early separation associated with delinquency.

⊖ Gender bias – weaker female superego is not supported by prison numbers.

⊖ Contradictory evidence – children without same-sex parent not less law-abiding.

⊖ Lack of falsifiability – unconscious concepts not open to empirical testing.

⊖ Problems with Bowlby's research – researcher bias, effects not inevitable (Koluchová).

⊖ Issues with causality – deprivation poor predictor of future offending (Lewis).

1 Psychodynamic theory is based on the concept of the:
(a) Inefficient superego.
(b) Inadequate superego.
(c) Inhibited superego.

2 *Not* a type of superego proposed by Blackburn:
(a) Weak.
(b) Immoral.
(c) Over-harsh.

3 What is this: Offending results from having a criminal same-sex parent?
(a) Deviant superego.
(b) Over-harsh superego.
(c) Weak superego.

4 The maternal deprivation hypothesis was proposed by:
(a) Belsky.
(b) Bowler.
(c) Bowlby.

5 Number of thieves in the deprivation study:
(a) 33
(b) 44
(c) 55

6 Superego develops in the:
(a) Phallic stage.
(b) Genital stage.
(c) Oral stage.

7 Found deprivation to be a poor predictor of future offending:
(a) Lillis.
(b) Lyons.
(c) Lewis.

8 Bowlby proposed that delinquency is linked to:
(a) Insecure-resistant attachment.
(b) Affectionless psychopathy.
(c) Having a criminal parent.

Topic 9: FORENSIC PSYCHOLOGY

Answers 1B 2B 3A 4C 5B 6A 7C 8B

Possible extended writing questions:
- Discuss **one** psychodynamic explanation and **one** cognitive explanation of offending. *[AL = 16]*
- Outline and evaluate psychodynamic explanations of offending. *[AL = 16]*

Book-link

Y2/A Student Book
Pages 338–339

Y2/A Revision Guide
Pages 220–221

Spec Spotlight

Dealing with offending behaviour: the aims of custodial sentencing and the psychological effects of custodial sentencing. Recidivism.

Aims of sentencing

Deterrence – put offender off crime, message to society.

Incapacitation – protect public by removing offender from society.

Retribution – society makes offender suffer as recompense.

Rehabilitation – reform of offender, learn new attitudes and life skills.

Psychological effects

Stress, depression, institutionalisation, prisonisation.

Recidivism

In UK 57% reoffend, rates vary according to offence and country.

⊖ Psychological effects of custodial sentencing – suicide, psychosis.

⊖ Individual differences – cannot assume all offenders react same way, different prisons differ.

⊕ Opportunity for rehabilitation – many access education and training.

⊖ Prisons can become 'universities of crime' – learn tricks of the trade.

⊖ Don't ignore alternatives to custodial sentencing – community service, restorative justice.

Topic 9: FORENSIC PSYCHOLOGY

1 Deterrence is *not*:
(a) Putting off the offender.
(b) Sending a message to society.
(c) Enacting revenge against the offender.

2 A weakness of custodial sentencing:
(a) Public feels dissatisfied.
(b) Retribution.
(c) Individual differences.

3 Another word for rehabilitation:
(a) Reform.
(b) Reoffend.
(c) Retire.

4 *Not* a psychological effect of prison:
(a) Institutionalisation.
(b) Individuation.
(c) Prisonisation.

5 Protecting the public by removing the offender:
(a) Incapability.
(b) Incapacitation.
(c) Incubation.

6 Reoffending rates in UK:
(a) 37%
(b) 47%
(c) 57%

7 Psychological effect of custodial sentencing:
(a) Loss of freedom.
(b) Prisonisation.
(c) Incapacitation.

8 An alternative to custodial sentencing:
(a) Community service.
(b) Community pride.
(c) Communal facilities.

Topic 9: FORENSIC PSYCHOLOGY

Answers
1C 2C 3A 4B
5B 6C 7B 8A

Possible extended writing questions:

- Discuss the aims of custodial sentencing. Refer to the issue of recidivism in your answer. *[AL = 16]*
- Discuss the psychological effects of custodial sentencing. *[AL = 16]*

Book-link

Y2/A Student Book
Pages 340–341

Y2/A Revision Guide
Pages 222–223

Spec Spotlight

Dealing with
offending behaviour:
behaviour modification
in custody.

AO1 Dealing with offending behaviour: Behaviour modification AO3

Behaviourist approach – undesirable behaviour is unlearned with conditioning.

Token economy – reinforce desirable behaviour, operant conditioning.

Tokens exchanged – for something desirable, e.g. cigarettes, food.

Tokens are secondary reinforcers – may be removed for disobedience (punishment).

Desirable behaviours are broken down into increments (small steps).

Prison staff – selectively and consistently reinforce identified behaviours.

⊕ Easy to implement – no specialists required but must be used consistently.

⊖ Little rehabilitative value – positive change lost outside prison (Blackburn).

⊖ Ethical issues – manipulative and dehumanising, may not be fair.

⊖ Learning is superficial – encourages passive learning of surface behaviour.

⊕ Individually tailored programmes can be effective (Field *et al.*).

Dealing with offending behaviour. Behaviour modification – *multiple choice questions*

1 The technique is based on the:
(a) Behaviourist approach.
(b) Cognitive approach.
(c) Psychodynamic approach.

2 Tokens are:
(a) Primary reinforcers.
(b) Secondary reinforcers.
(c) Tertiary reinforcers.

3 The rewarding of desirable behaviour is based on:
(a) Classical conditioning.
(b) Vicarious conditioning.
(c) Operant conditioning.

4 Breaking down of behaviour into small steps is:
(a) Increments.
(b) Implements.
(c) Instalments.

5 In a token economy disobedient behaviour may lead to the:
(a) Renewal of tokens.
(b) Removal of tokens.
(c) Return of tokens.

6 Claimed that behaviour modification had little rehabilitative value:
(a) Blackburn.
(b) Blackwell.
(c) Blackwood.

7 Found evidence for the success of individually tailored programmes:
(a) Lake *et al.*
(b) Wood *et al.*
(c) Field *et al.*

8 One strength of behaviour modification:
(a) No ethical issues.
(b) Long lasting.
(c) Easy to implement.

Answers
1A 2B 3C 4A
5B 6A 7C 8C

Topic 9: FORENSIC PSYCHOLOGY

Possible extended writing questions:

- Discuss **one** method used to deal with offending behaviour. *[AL = 16]*
- Outline and evaluate the use of behaviour modification in custody. *[AL = 16]*

Dealing with offending behaviour: Anger management

AO1

Book-link

Y2/A Student Book
Pages 342–343

Y2/A Revision Guide
Pages 224–225

Spec Spotlight

Dealing with
offending behaviour:
anger management.

Cognition triggers emotions first – and they trigger aggressive acts (Novaco).

CBT – teach offenders to recognise anger, and gives them skills to deal with it.

Stage 1: Cognitive preparation – identify the triggers to anger.

Stage 2: Skill acquisition – techniques to deal with anger, e.g. self-talk, meditation.

Stage 3: Application practice – role play skills in a monitored environment.

Positive outcomes with young offenders – increased awareness of anger and increased self-control (Keen *et al.*).

AO3

⊕ An eclectic approach – cognitive, behavioural, social, acknowledges complexity.

⊕ Tries to tackle causes – thought processes underlying offending.

⊖ Long-term effectiveness poor – short-term effects but limited long term (Blackburn).

⊖ Anger may not be the cause – violent and non-violent offenders equally aggressive (Loza and Loza-Fanous).

⊖ Expensive and commitment required – many prisons cannot fund it.

1 Which order is correct?
(a) Emotion → aggression → cognition.
(b) Aggression → cognition → emotion.
(c) Cognition → emotion → aggression.

2 Role play skills in a monitored environment:
(a) Cognitive preparation.
(b) Skill acquisition.
(c) Application practice.

3 Cognitive preparation involves:
(a) Identifying barriers to anger.
(b) Identifying triggers to anger.
(c) Identifying solutions to anger.

4 *Not* a technique used to deal with anger in CBT:
(a) Self-talk.
(b) Meditation.
(c) Violence.

5 Found increased awareness of anger and self-control:
(a) Queen *et al.*
(b) Keen *et al.*
(c) Green *et al.*

6 A strength of anger management:
(a) Long-term effectiveness.
(b) Eclectic approach.
(c) Relatively inexpensive method.

7 Found evidence that anger may *not* be the cause of offending:
(a) Liza and Liza-Fanous.
(b) Leeza and Leeza-Fanous.
(c) Loza and Loza-Fanous.

8 Approach *not* part of anger management:
(a) Behavioural.
(b) Psychodynamic.
(c) Cognitive.

Answers
1C 2C 3B 4C
5B 6A 7C 8B

Topic 9: FORENSIC PSYCHOLOGY

Possible extended writing questions:
- Discuss **one or more** ways of dealing with offending behaviour. *[AL = 16]*
- Outline and evaluate anger management as a way of dealing with offenders. *[AL = 16]*

Dealing with offending behaviour: Restorative justice

Book-link

Y2/A Student Book
Pages 344–345

Y2/A Revision Guide
Pages 226–227

Spec Spotlight

Dealing with
offending behaviour:
restorative justice
programmes.

AO1

Crime is against individual – rather than against the state, so switch emphasis.

Victims take an active role – offenders see the consequences of their actions.

Healing process – victim explains emotional impact, managed collaboration.

Key features – focus on acceptance, non-courtroom setting, active, positive outcomes.

Some variations – e.g. not face-to-face, financial restitution, fixing damage.

Restorative Justice Council (RJC) establishes standards and promotes use.

AO3

⊕ Diversity of RJ programmes – applications in schools, hospitals, etc.

⊖ Relies on the offender showing remorse – some sign up for reduced sentence.

⊖ May not be cost-effective – for every £1 spent, £8 saved by reducing offending (Shapland *et al.*) but requires skilled mediator.

⊖ Feminist critique of RJ – power imbalance in domestic violence cases.

⊖ Seen as a 'soft option' – despite being cheaper and reducing recidivism.

Dealing with offending behaviour: Restorative justice – *multiple choice questions*

1 RJ emphasises that crime is committed against:
(a) The individual.
(b) The state.
(c) The community.

2 The victim is encouraged to take:
(a) A passive role.
(b) An active role.
(c) A backseat role.

6 *Not* a principle of RJ:
(a) Collaboration.
(b) Economic.
(c) Healing.

4 RJC stands for:
(a) Restorative Justice Corporation.
(b) Restorative Justice Council.
(c) Restorative Justice Company.

5 Victim enables offender to see:
(a) The consequences of their actions.
(b) That they must not offend again.
(c) The physical damage done.

6 A variant of RJ:
(a) Custodial sentence.
(b) Anger management.
(c) Financial restitution.

7 Estimates suggest that for every £1 spent on RJ:
(a) £6 is saved.
(b) £7 is saved.
(c) £8 is saved.

8 A strength of RJ:
(a) Offenders always show remorse.
(b) Programmes are diverse.
(c) Support from feminist groups.

Answers
1A 2B 3B 4B
5A 6C 7C 8B

Possible extended writing questions:

• Discuss **two or more** ways of dealing with offending behaviour. *[AL = 16]*
• Outline and evaluate restorative justice as a method of dealing with offending behaviour. *[AL = 16]*

Book-link

Y2/A Student Book
Page 356

Y2/A Revision Guide
Pages 228–229

Spec Spotlight

Describing
addiction: physical
and psychological
dependence, tolerance
and withdrawal
syndrome.

AO1

Describing addiction

Dependence

Physical – happens when withdrawal symptoms occur after abstaining from a drug.

Psychological – compulsion to experience effects of a drug to increase pleasure or reduce discomfort, becomes habit.

Tolerance

Response to usual dose is reduced – greater dose needed for same effect.

Cross-tolerance – tolerance to one drug reduces sensitivity to another (e.g. alcohol and anaesthetic).

Withdrawal syndrome

Collection of symptoms develop after abstinence – usually opposite to desired effects.

Sign of physical dependence – symptoms experienced when drug not available, take drug to avoid symptoms.

1 Addiction can occur to:
(a) A chemical substance.
(b) A behaviour.
(c) Both of the above.

2 The three main features of addiction are:
(a) Tolerance, physical dependence, psychological dependence.
(b) Dependence, tolerance, withdrawal syndrome.
(c) Tolerance, withdrawal, pleasure.

3 Someone is physically dependent on a drug when they:
(a) Crave the pleasurable effects.
(b) Have withdrawal after stopping.
(c) Develop tolerance.

4 Psychological dependence is:
(a) Compulsory.
(b) Compensatory.
(c) A compulsion.

5 Tolerance to a drug occurs when:
(a) More is needed for a greater effect.
(b) More is needed for the same effect.
(c) Less is needed for the same effect.

6 A special form of tolerance is:
(a) Cross-tolerance.
(b) Angry-tolerance.
(c) Furious-tolerance.

7 Withdrawal syndrome occurs when the addict:
(a) Increases the dose of a drug.
(b) Stops taking a drug.
(c) Starts taking the drug after a period of abstinence.

8 The symptoms of withdrawal are:
(a) Similar to effects of the drug.
(b) Opposite to effects of the drug.
(c) Usually pleasurable.

Answers
1C 2B 3B 4C
5B 6A 7B 8B

Possible extended writing questions:

- Explain the difference between physical dependence and psychological dependence in relation to addiction. *[AL = 4]*
- Briefly outline features of addiction. *[AL = 6]*

AO1

AO3

Book-link

Y2/A Student Book
Page 357–359

Y2/A Revision Guide
Pages 230–231

Spec Spotlight

Risk factors
in the development
of addiction, including
genetic vulnerability,
stress, personality,
family influences
and peers.

Genetic vulnerability – e.g. low numbers of dopamine D2 receptors inherited.

Stress – early trauma linked to addiction, damage to brain in sensitive period.

Personality – antisocial personality disorder, impulsivity may have shared genetic basis with addiction.

Family influences – perceived parental approval and exposure (drinking as part of family life).

Peers – rule-breaking norms within peer group, peers provide opportunities.

⊕ Research support for genes – adopted child at greater risk if biological parent is an addict (Kendler et al.).

⊕ Genes explain indirect effects – e.g. lack of self-control partly genetic.

⊖ Factors interact – combinations of factors determine addiction, not single.

⊖ Cause and effect – risk factors and addiction are correlated, not causal.

⊕ Real-life application – identifying factors can lead to interventions (e.g. resisting peer pressure, Tobler et al.).

Risk factors in the development of addictions – *multiple choice questions*

1 Low numbers of dopamine receptors is an example of:
(a) Genetic vulnerability.
(b) Stress.
(c) A personality factor.

2 Stress is a risk factor mainly in the form of:
(a) Antisocial personality.
(b) Parental approval of alcohol.
(c) Childhood trauma.

3 The personality trait most risky for addiction is:
(a) Impulsivity.
(b) Introversion.
(c) Openness.

4 Excessive alcohol intake in adolescence is linked to:
(a) Parental disapproval.
(b) Perceived parental approval.
(c) Peer disapproval.

5 The strongest support for genetics as a risk factor comes from:
(a) Studies of early childhood trauma.
(b) Studies of personality.
(c) Adoption studies.

6 _____ is indirectly linked to addiction.
(a) A lack of dopamine.
(b) A low number of D2 receptors.
(c) Self-control.

7 The most likely explanation of addiction is:
(a) A combination of risk factors.
(b) One factor is more important than the others.
(c) Stress is least influential.

8 Risk factors are:
(a) Direct causes of addiction.
(b) Correlated with addiction.
(c) Indirect causes of addiction.

Answers
1A 2C 3A 4B
5C 6C 7A 8B

Possible extended writing questions:

- Discuss genetic vulnerability **and** family influences as risk factors in the development of addiction. *[AL = 16]*
- Outline and evaluate **two or more** risk factors in the development of addiction. *[AL = 16]*

Book-link

Y2/A Student Book
Page 360–361

Y2/A Revision Guide
Pages 232–233

Spec Spotlight

Explanations for
nicotine addiction:
brain neurochemistry,
including the role of
dopamine.

A01 Explanations for nicotine addiction: Brain neurochemistry **A03**

Role of dopamine

Desensitisation hypothesis – nAChRs (nicotinic receptors) respond to nicotine in ventral tegmental area (VTA).

Desensitisation – nicotine binds to nAChR, neuron produces dopamine, then shuts down.

Dopamine – released along VTA to nucleus accumbens and frontal cortex, creates reward.

Nicotine regulation model

Abstain from smoking, nAChRs re-sensitise.

Upregulation leads to withdrawal – smoking avoids withdrawal, maintained.

Chronic desensitisation – fewer active receptors, more nicotine needed, therefore tolerance.

⊕ Supporting evidence – haloperidol increases smoking in schizophrenics, to increase dopamine (McEvoy *et al.*).

⊕ Real-life application – NRT based on knowledge of neurochemistry.

⊖ Not just dopamine – highly complex, GABA and serotonin involved.

⊖ Reductionist – ignores social-psychological influences (e.g. peers).

⊖ Individual differences – 'chippers' do not become dependent, non-chemical explanation (e.g. modelling).

Explanations for nicotine addiction: Brain neurochemistry – multiple choice questions

1 Nicotinic receptors (nAChRs) are found in the:
(a) Nucleus accumbens.
(b) Ventral tegmental area.
(c) Hypothalamus.

2 Dopamine travels along pathways to the:
(a) Nucleus accumbens.
(b) Frontal cortex.
(c) Both of the above.

3 When a smoker abstains from smoking:
(a) Downregulation occurs.
(b) nAChRs become re-sensitised.
(c) nAChRs are destroyed.

4 Chronic desensitisation of nAChRs means that a smoker:
(a) Needs more nicotine.
(b) Smokes less.
(c) Has more active nAChRs.

5 Haloperidol increases smoking in schizophrenics because smoking:
(a) Increases dopamine.
(b) Decreases dopamine.
(c) Is a symptom of schizophrenia.

6 Brain neurochemistry of nicotine addiction also involves:
(a) GABA only.
(b) GABA and serotonin.
(c) Serotonin only.

7 Brain neurochemistry ignores psychological factors and therefore is:
(a) Based on nurture.
(b) Determinist.
(c) Reductionist.

8 'Chippers' contradict the neurochemistry explanation because:
(a) They do not smoke.
(b) They do not become dependent.
(c) They are addicted.

Answers 1B 2C 3B 4A 5A 6B 7C 8B

Possible extended writing questions:
- Describe and evaluate **one or more** explanations for nicotine addiction. *[AL = 16]*
- Discuss brain neurochemistry as an explanation for nicotine addiction. Refer to the role of dopamine in your answer. *[AL = 16]*

Book-link

Y2/A Student Book
Page 362–363

Y2/A Revision Guide
Pages 234–235

Spec Spotlight

Explanations for nicotine addiction: learning theory as applied to smoking behaviour, including reference to cue reactivity.

Topic 10: ADDICTION

Operant conditioning

Smoking creates mild euphoria, positive reinforcement.

Mild euphoria – nicotine stimulates release of dopamine in mesolimbic pathway.

Negative reinforcement – smoking avoids unpleasant withdrawal symptoms.

Classical conditioning

Smoking is a primary reinforcer because intrinsically rewarding (not learned).

Secondary reinforcers – rewarding via association with primary reinforcer.

Cue reactivity

Secondary reinforcers, smoking-related cues triggering cravings.

⊕ Support from animal studies – rats lick nicotine water spout, effects reinforce preference (Levin *et al.*).

⊕ Support for cue reactivity – cue exposure linked to cravings and arousal (Carter and Tiffany).

⊕ Real-life application – aversion therapy counter-conditions nicotine addiction.

⊕ Gender differences – females less likely to quit because more sensitive to smoking-related cues.

⊖ Some not addicted – despite same reinforcements not everyone dependent.

Explanations for nicotine addiction: Learning theory – *multiple choice questions*

1 Smokers continue smoking because mild euphoria:
(a) Negatively reinforces smoking.
(b) Is a cue.
(c) Positively reinforces smoking.

2 The neurotransmitter most stimulated by nicotine is:
(a) Adrenaline.
(b) Dopamine.
(c) Serotonin.

3 Smoking is a primary reinforcer because:
(a) Its effects are learned.
(b) It is intrinsically rewarding.
(c) We learn it in school.

4 Secondary reinforcer that triggers nicotine cravings is:
(a) Cue reactivity.
(b) Negative reinforcement.
(c) Operant conditioning.

5 Effects of nicotine reinforce licking of a nicotine waterspout in:
(a) Humans.
(b) Rats.
(c) All non-human animals.

6 A real-life application of learning theory is:
(a) Aversion therapy.
(b) Cognitive behaviour therapy.
(c) Drug treatment.

7 Women are less likely than men to quit smoking because they are:
(a) Harder to condition.
(b) Less sensitive to smoking cues.
(c) More sensitive to smoking cues.

8 Carter and Tiffany found that exposure to smoking cues is linked to:
(a) Physiological arousal only.
(b) Psychological cravings only.
(c) Both of the above.

Topic 10: ADDICTION

Answers
1C 2B 3B 4A
5B 6A 7C 8C

Possible extended writing questions:

- Discuss **two** explanations for nicotine addiction. *[AL = 16]*
- Outline and evaluate learning theory as applied to smoking behaviour. Refer to cue reactivity in your answer. *[AL = 16]*

Explanations for gambling addiction: Learning theory

AO1 | **AO3**

Book-link

Y2/A Student Book
Page 364–365

Y2/A Revision Guide
Pages 236–237

Spec Spotlight

Explanations for
gambling addiction:
learning theory as
applied to gambling,
including reference to
partial and variable
reinforcement.

AO1

Vicarious reinforcement – observing others being rewarded for gambling.

Direct reinforcement – positive if direct gain, negative if from distraction.

Partial reinforcement – only some gambles pay off, unpredictable.

Variable reinforcement – variable ratio schedule most powerful in gambling.

Variable reinforcement – means gambling behaviour very resistant to extinction.

Cue reactivity – secondary reinforcers associated with arousal, trigger gambling.

AO3

⊕ Research support – high-frequency gamblers place last-minute bets, delay excitement (Dickerson).

⊖ Lack of explanatory power – explains some gambling better than others (e.g. games of chance).

⊖ Individual differences – different responses to conditioning hard to explain without cognitive features.

⊖ Not all aspects – hard to explain start of gambling, thus incomplete explanation.

⊕ Explains failure to stop – motivational forces keep gambler addicted.

Explanations for gambling addiction: Learning theory — *multiple choice questions*

1 Gambling because you observe others being rewarded is:
(a) Positive reinforcement.
(b) Negative reinforcement.
(c) Vicarious reinforcement.

2 Gambling to avoid the anxieties of everyday life occurs through:
(a) Positive reinforcement.
(b) Negative reinforcement.
(c) Partial reinforcement.

3 In a partial reinforcement schedule:
(a) Only some gambles are rewarded.
(b) Rewards are very predictable.
(c) Extinction occurs quickly.

4 Gambling reinforced through a variable ratio schedule:
(a) Is resistant to extinction.
(b) Is vicarious.
(c) Does not lead to relapse.

5 Frequent gamblers are more likely than occasional gamblers to:
(a) Win.
(b) Place bets at the last minute.
(c) Stop gambling after losing.

6 Learning is a good explanation of gambling on games:
(a) Without immediate rewards.
(b) With chance outcomes.
(c) Of skill.

7 Learning theory struggles to explain individual differences:
(a) In terms of conditioning.
(b) Without using cognitive factors.
(c) In terms of cue reactivity.

8 Learning theory is relatively weak at explaining:
(a) How gambling addiction begins.
(b) How gambling addiction stops.
(c) Relapse into gambling addiction.

Answers
1C 2B 3A 4A
5B 6C 7B 8A

Topic 10: ADDICTION

Possible extended writing questions:

• Outline and evaluate **one or more** explanations for gambling addiction. *[AL = 16]*
• Discuss learning theory as applied to gambling. Refer in your answer to partial **and** variable reinforcement. *[AL = 16]*

AO1

Explanations for gambling addiction: Cognitive theory

AO3

Expectancy theory – expected benefits outweigh costs, not conscious decision.

Cognitive bias – irrational, selective information processing (e.g. attention).

Categories of bias – skill/judgement, personal traits/ritual behaviours, selective recall, faulty perceptions.

Relapse – occurs through lack of self-efficacy ('Told you I couldn't give up').

Key study: Griffiths

Procedure – 'thinking aloud', content analysis as rational or irrational.

Findings – regular gamblers 6 times more irrational utterances than controls.

(+) Research support – addicted gamblers have more distorted cognitions (Michalczuk *et al.*).

(+) Explains automatic behaviour – using Stroop, cognitive bias towards gambling words (McCusker and Gettings).

(−) Individual differences – personality a factor, not just cognitive biases.

(+) Real-life application – CBT to change addicted gamblers' distorted thinking.

(−) Methodological issues – self-reports may not represent true beliefs.

Spec Spotlight

Explanations for gambling addiction: cognitive theory as applied to gambling, including reference to cognitive bias.

1 Gamblers' cognitions about gambling are:
(a) Irrational.
(b) Unbiased.
(c) Logical.

2 One of the four categories of cognitive bias is:
(a) Genetic predispositions.
(b) Distorted personality.
(c) Faulty perceptions.

3 Gamblers relapse because:
(a) They are moral failures.
(b) No therapy works.
(c) They lack self-efficacy.

4 Griffiths used the _____ method to study cognitive biases.
(a) Questionnaire.
(b) Thinking aloud.
(c) Correlational.

5 One method of studying cognitive biases in gambling addicts uses:
(a) The Bloop procedure.
(b) The Gloop procedure.
(c) The Stroop procedure.

6 An example of selective information processing in gambling is:
(a) Attention.
(b) Classical conditioning.
(c) Personality factors.

7 A real-life application of the theory to gambling addiction is:
(a) CBT.
(b) Drug therapy.
(c) Genetic engineering.

8 Self-report methods in gambling studies:
(a) Are objective and unbiased.
(b) May not represent true beliefs.
(c) Are rarely used.

Answers
1A 2C 3C 4B
5C 6A 7A 8B

Possible extended writing questions:
- Discuss **two** explanations for gambling addiction. *[AL = 16]*
- Describe and evaluate cognitive theory as applied to gambling. Refer to cognitive bias in your answer. *[AL = 16]*

Reducing addiction: Drug therapy

Book-link

Y2/A Student Book
Page 368–369

Y2/A Revision Guide
Pages 240–241

Spec Spotlight

Reducing addiction:
drug therapy.

AO1

Aversive drugs – classical conditioning, pair alcohol with unpleasant effects.

Agonists – activate neurons, replace addictive drug, produce similar effects.

Antagonists – block neuron receptors to prevent the effects of addictive drug.

Smoking – NRT stimulates controlled dopamine release, avoids withdrawal.

Gambling – opioid antagonists increase GABA, reduce dopamine, control craving.

Use of drugs – no drugs officially approved for gambling addiction (side effects).

AO3

⊕ Research support – NRT better than placebo to quit smoking (Stead *et al.*).

⊖ Side effects – risk of discontinuing treatment, weigh up against benefits.

⊖ Requires motivation – best suited to just a very small subset of addicts.

⊕ No stigma – drug therapy shows addiction is a medical issue, not moral failing.

⊖ Individual differences – genetic variations affect treatment success.

1 Aversive drugs work through the process of:
(a) Operant conditioning.
(b) Classical conditioning.
(c) Vicarious reinforcement.

2 Drugs that produce similar effects to addictive substances are:
(a) Antagonists.
(b) Agonists.
(c) Aversives.

3 Antagonists work by:
(a) Blocking neuron receptors.
(b) Activating neurons.
(c) Enhancing neuron receptors.

4 Opioid antagonists help gambling addiction by:
(a) Increasing dopamine release.
(b) Reducing GABA release.
(c) Reducing dopamine release.

5 NRT is an effective therapy for smoking addiction because:
(a) There are no side effects.
(b) Everyone who uses it quits.
(c) It's better than placebo.

6 Perhaps the biggest problem with side effects of a drug is:
(a) The addict will stop treatment.
(b) They stop the treatment working.
(c) No-one knows what they are.

7 Drug treatment requires motivation, so:
(a) Every addict can benefit from it.
(b) It's convenient and easy.
(c) It suits a limited group of addicts.

8 Most psychologists would probably agree that addiction is:
(a) The fault of the addict.
(b) A moral failing.
(c) Associated with stigma.

Answers
1B 2B 3A 4C
5C 6A 7C 8C

Possible extended writing questions:

- Discuss **one** method of reducing addiction. *[AL = 16]*
- Describe and evaluate drug therapy as a method of reducing addiction. *[AL = 16]*

Book-link

Y2/A Student Book
Page 370–371

Y2/A Revision Guide
Pages 242–243

Spec Spotlight

Reducing addiction: behavioural interventions, including aversion therapy and covert sensitisation.

Aversion therapy

Associates addiction with unpleasant consequences.

Disulfiram – plus drinking alcohol causes severe instant nausea and vomiting.

Electric shocks – given when read gambling-related phrase, UCR is pain.

⊖ Methodological problems – inbuilt biases (e.g. not 'blinded'), lacks validity (Hajek and Stead).

⊖ Treatment adherence – stressful therapy so high drop-out, hard to judge effectiveness.

⊖ Short-term – long-term effects of aversion no better than placebo (McConaghy *et al.*).

Covert sensitisation

In vitro, i.e. unpleasant stimulus imagined.

Nicotine – imagine smoking and horrible effects, associate two mentally.

Techniques – imagined stimuli chosen by client (e.g. faeces), also imagine relief afterwards.

⊕ Research support – 90% reduction in gambling after 1 year, 30% for aversion (McConaghy *et al.*).

⊕ Ethical issues – no vomiting or self-shaming (as in aversion), client retains dignity.

1 Aversion therapy is based on:
(a) Negative reinforcement.
(b) Modelling.
(c) Classical conditioning.

2 The UCS used to treat gambling is usually:
(a) Electric shocks.
(b) A drug.
(c) Extreme heat.

3 Covert sensitisation is:
(a) In vivo.
(b) In vimto.
(c) In vitro.

4 In covert sensitisation, the aversive stimuli are always:
(a) Chosen by the therapist.
(b) Highly repulsive.
(c) Enjoyable and pleasant.

5 Many studies of aversion therapy lack validity because they:
(a) Have a control group.
(b) Have methodological limitations.
(c) Show that it doesn't work.

6 'Treatment adherence' as an issue in aversion therapy means:
(a) Many people drop out.
(b) The therapy is highly effective.
(c) There are no ethical issues.

7 Aversion therapy is effective:
(a) Only in the short term.
(b) Short term and long term.
(c) Not even in the short term.

8 Ethically, covert sensitisation is:
(a) Unproblematic.
(b) Unacceptable.
(c) Preferable to aversion therapy.

Answers
1C 2A 3C 4B
5B 6A 7A 8C

Possible extended writing questions:
- Outline and evaluate **one or more** behavioural interventions as methods of reducing addiction. [AL = 16]
- Discuss aversion therapy **and/or** covert sensitisation as methods of reducing addiction. [AL = 16]

Reducing addiction: Cognitive behaviour therapy

Book-link

Y2/A Student Book
Page 372–373

Y2/A Revision Guide
Pages 244–245

Spec Spotlight

Reducing addiction:
cognitive behaviour
therapy.

Main aims – to tackle client's distorted thinking and develop coping behaviours.

(1) *Cognitive* functional analysis – identify high-risk situations, therapist challenges.

(2) *Behaviour* skills training – client learns to replace poor coping skills with adaptive ones.

Developing new skills – cognitive restructuring, challenge faulty beliefs.

Specific skills – apply to wider life, e.g. anger management, assertiveness.

Social skills training – cope with anxiety in social situations (e.g. refuse alcohol).

⊕ Research support – CBT group gambled less than controls after 12 months (Petry *et al.*).

⊖ Not long term – other studies show CBT only effective up to 3 months (Cowlishaw *et al.*).

⊖ Treatment adherence – relatively high drop-out rate, challenging therapy.

⊕ Relapse prevention – relapse not sign of failure, acceptable part of progress.

⊖ Hard to identify key element – flexibility is a strength but not clear what works.

Reducing addiction: Cognitive behaviour therapy – multiple choice questions

1 **CBT begins with:**
   (a) Learning coping techniques.
   (b) A cognitive functional analysis.
   (c) Applying coping techniques.

2 **The behavioural element of CBT is:**
   (a) Feeling better about gambling.
   (b) Thinking rationally about gambling.
   (c) Use adaptive coping methods.

3 **Challenging the client's faulty beliefs is:**
   (a) Part of skills training.
   (b) Not part of CBT.
   (c) Part of cognitive restructuring.

4 **One form of specific skills training is:**
   (a) Functional analysis.
   (b) Anger management.
   (c) Social skills training.

5 **CBT is most effective in reducing addiction for up to ___ months.**
   (a) 3
   (b) 6
   (c) 12

6 **CBT has a relatively high drop-out rate because:**
   (a) Most gamblers are lazy.
   (b) It doesn't work.
   (c) It is a challenging therapy.

7 **In CBT, relapse is seen as:**
   (a) A personal catastrophe.
   (b) A bit of a laugh.
   (c) An inevitable part of recovery.

8 **It is unclear how CBT works because:**
   (a) All CBT programmes are the same.
   (b) It includes many techniques.
   (c) It is inflexible.

Answers
1B 2C 3C 4B
5A 6C 7C 8B

Possible extended writing questions:

- Describe and evaluate **two or more** methods of reducing addiction. *[AL = 16]*
- Outline and evaluate cognitive behaviour therapy as a method of reducing addiction. *[AL = 16]*

A01

Applying the theory of planned behaviour

A03

Intention to change – central, must be deliberate, linked to 3 key influences.

(1) Personal attitudes – favourable and unfavourable, towards addiction.

(2) Subjective norms – what do key people in the addict's life believe is normal?

What matters – the addict's *perception* of these people's approval/disapproval.

(3) Perceived behavioural control – self-efficacy, addict's belief they can stop.

Control is direct (tries hard to stop) and indirect (influences intention to stop).

⊕ Research support – depends on addiction (good support for alcohol, Hagger *et al.*).

⊖ Intention-behaviour gap – little support for predicting behaviour from intentions (Miller and Howell).

⊖ Doesn't predict long-term changes – intentions only predict change within five weeks (McEachan *et al.*).

⊖ Methodological issues – correlations, intentions do not cause change.

⊖ Assumes rationality – theory assumes that people make rational decisions.

Spec Spotlight

The application of the following theory of behaviour change to addictive behaviour; the theory of planned behaviour.

Applying the theory of planned behaviour – multiple choice questions

1 The central feature of the theory is:
(a) Control over behaviour.
(b) Personal attitudes to addiction.
(c) The intention to change.

2 'Addict's perception of approval from key people' refers to:
(a) Intentions to change.
(b) Subjective norms.
(c) Perceived behavioural control.

3 The addict's belief that they are able to give up their addiction is:
(a) Self-efficacy.
(b) Self-confidence.
(c) Self-esteem.

4 The influence of perceived behavioural control is:
(a) Direct only.
(b) Indirect only.
(c) Both direct and indirect.

5 Research supports the theory in relation to _____ addiction.
(a) Sex.
(b) Alcohol.
(c) Gambling.

6 In reality it is hard to predict behaviour from:
(a) Intentions.
(b) Attitudes.
(c) Norms.

7 The theory can only predict change from intentions within:
(a) Five weeks.
(b) Five months.
(c) Five years.

8 The theory assumes people make decisions:
(a) Illogically.
(b) Based on biases.
(c) Rationally.

Answers
1C 2B 3A 4C
5B 6A 7A 8C

Possible extended writing questions:
- Discuss how **one** theory of behaviour change can be applied to addictive behaviour. *[AL = 16]*
- Describe and evaluate the theory of planned behaviour in relation to addictive behaviour. *[AL = 16]*

AO1

AO3

Topic 10: ADDICTION

Book-link

Y2/A Student Book
Page 376–377

Y2/A Revision Guide
Pages 248–249

Spec Spotlight

The application of the following theory of behaviour change to addictive behaviour; Prochaska's six-stage model of behaviour change.

Six-stage model – each stage represents differing readiness to change (dynamic).

(1) Pre-contemplation – not thinking of change in next six months.

(2) Contemplation – thinking of a change in next six months, aware of costs/benefits.

(3) Preparation – making change in the next month, but not decided how to do this.

(4) Action – done something (formal or informal) to change in last six months.

(5) Maintenance – change has continued for six months, focus on relapse prevention.

(6) Termination – abstinence is automatic, relapse unlikely, not realistic for everyone.

⊕ True nature of addiction – dynamic, continuing process over time, stages.

⊖ Contradictory research – 'the model should be discarded' (West).

⊖ Arbitrary stages – e.g. stages 1 and 2 not qualitatively different (why 30 days?).

⊕ Attitude to relapse – realistic, takes it seriously but viewed as part of process.

⊖ Lacks predictive validity – unable to predict who seeks change at each stage.

1 Someone considering making a change in next six months is in the:
(a) Pre-contemplation stage.
(b) Preparation stage.
(c) Contemplation stage.

2 Changing behaviour in the last six months means you are in the:
(a) Preparation stage.
(b) Action stage.
(c) Termination stage.

3 Preventing relapse is the focus of the:
(a) Maintenance stage.
(b) Action stage.
(c) Preparation stage.

4 It is unrealistic to expect everyone to reach the:
(a) Preparation stage.
(b) Pre-contemplation stage.
(c) Termination stage.

5 The model assumes that behaviour change is:
(a) An 'all-or-nothing' event.
(b) A dynamic process over time.
(c) A passive, static process.

6 West believes that Prochaska's model:
(a) Is the best thing ever.
(b) Should be discarded.
(c) Is no better or worse than others.

7 'Stages are arbitrary' means that stages 1 and 2:
(a) Do not really exist.
(b) Are not all that different.
(c) Should be abandoned.

8 The model views relapse as:
(a) Part of the change process.
(b) A personal failure.
(c) Something to be encouraged.

Answers
1C 2B 3A 4C
5B 6B 7B 8A

Topic 10: ADDICTION

Possible extended writing questions:
- Outline and evaluate the application of **two** theories of behaviour change to addictive behaviour. *[AL = 16]*
- Discuss Prochaska's six-stage model of behaviour change in relation to addictive behaviour. *[AL = 16]*

NOTES

NOTES

NOTES